D0596110

genesis

the first book of moses, called

genesis

authorized king james version

grove press
new york

with an introduction by | e. l. doctorow

*The Pocket Canons were originally published in the U.K. in 1998 by
Canongate Books, Ltd.*
Published simultaneously in Canada
Printed in the United States of America

FIRST AMERICAN EDITION

Copyright information is on file with the Library of Congress
ISBN 0-8021-3610-9

Design by Paddy Cramsie

Grove Press
841 Broadway
New York, NY 10003

99 00 01 02   10 9 8 7 6 5 4 3 2 1

a note about pocket canons

The Authorized King James Version of the Bible, translated between 1603 and 1611, coincided with an extraordinary flowering of English literature. This version, more than any other, and possibly more than any other work in history, has had an influence in shaping the language we speak and write today. Presenting individual books from the Bible as separate volumes, as they were originally conceived, encourages the reader to approach them as literary works in their own right.

The first twelve books in this series encompass categories as diverse as history, fiction, philosophy, love poetry, and law. Each Pocket Canon also has its own introduction, specially commissioned from an impressive range of writers, which provides a personal interpretation of the text and explores its contemporary relevance.

E. L. Doctorow's books include the novels Ragtime, Billy Bathgate, Loon Lake, *and* The Book of Daniel. *His work has won two National Book Critics Circle Awards, the National Book Award, the PEN/Faulkner Award, the Edith Wharton citation for fiction, and the William Dean Howells medal from the American Academy of Arts and Letters. He lives and works in New York City.*

introduction by e. l. doctorow

The King James Version of The Bible, an early-seventeenth-century translation, seems, by its now venerable diction, to have added a degree of poetic luster to the ancient tales, genealogies, and covenantal events of the original. It is the version preachers quote from who believe in the divinity of the text.

Certainly in the case of Genesis 1–4, in which the world is formed and populated and Adam and Eve are sent from the Garden, there could be no more appropriate language than the English of Shakespeare's time. The King James does not suffer at all from what is inconsistent or self-contradictory in the text any more than do the cryptic ancient Hebrew and erring Greek from which it is derived. Once you assume poetically divine authorship, only your understanding is imperfect.

But when you read of these same matters in the contemporary diction of the English Revised Bible, the Jamesian voice of Holy Scripture is not quite what you hear. In plain-spoken modern English, Genesis—especially as it moves on from the Flood and the Tower of Babel, and comes up in time through the lives of Abraham, Sarah, Isaac, Rebecca, and then to the more detailed adventures of Jacob and Rachel and Joseph and his brothers—seems manifestly of the oral tradition of preliterate storytelling out of which the biblical documents emerged, when history and moral instruction, genealogy, law, science, and momentous confrontations with God were not recorded on papyrus or clay tablets but held in the mind for transmittal by generations of narrators. And so Genesis in the English Revised Version is homier—something like a collection of stories about people trying to work things out.

The contemporary reader would do well to read the King James herein side by side with the English Revised. Some lovely stereophonic truths come of the fact that a devotion to God did not preclude the use of narrative strategies.

If not in all stories, certainly in all mystery stories, the writer works backward. The ending is known and the story is designed to arrive at the ending. If you know the people of the world speak many languages, that is the ending: The story of the Tower of Babel gets you there. The known ending of life is death: The story of Adam and Eve, and the forbidden fruit of the Tree of the Knowledge of Good and Evil, arrives at that ending. Why do we suffer, why must we die? Well, you see, there was this Garden. . . . The story has turned the human condition into a sequential narrative of how it came to be; it has used conflict and suspense to create a moral framework for *being*. And in suggesting that things might have worked out another way for humanity if the fruit had not been eaten, it has, not incidentally, left itself open to revision by some subsequent fantasist who will read into it the idea of original sin.

Artistry is at work also in the blessings the dying Jacob bestows on his twelve eponymous sons. Each blessing, an astute judgment of character, will explain the fate of the twelve tribes led by the sons. A beginning is invented for each of the historical tribal endings the writer knows. Never mind that we understand from the documentary thesis of Bible sources—for it is, after all, the work of various storytellers and their editors—that different sons are accorded hands-on leadership by their father according to which writer is telling the story. Character is fate. And life under God is always an allegory.

Another venerable storytelling practice is the appropriation of an already existing story. Otherwise known as adaptation, it is the principle of literary communalism that allows us to use other people's myths, legends, and histories in the way that serves ourselves—Shakespeare's reliance on Hollinshed's Chronicles, for example, which should have, in honor, disposed him to share his royalites. Here in Genesis, the ancient scribes have retooled the story of the Flood recounted earlier in Mesopotamia and Sumer, including the vivid rendition in the Epic of Gilgamesh. Yet though the plot is the same, the resounding meanings are different, as befits an adaptation. Noah is unprecedented as the last godfearing, righteous man on earth . . . who may nevertheless drink a bit more wine than is good for him. And the God of Genesis is a Presence beyond the conception of the Sumerian epic.

The cosmology of Genesis is beautiful and, for all we know, may even turn out to be as metaphorically prescient as some believers think it is. One imagines the ancient storytellers convening to consider what they had to work with: day and night, land and sea, earth and sky, trees that bore fruit, plants that bore seed, wild animals, domesticated animals, birds, fish, and everything that crept. In their brilliant imaginations, inflamed by the fear and love of God, it seemed more than possible that these elements and forms of life, this organization of the animate and inanimate, would have been produced from a chaos of indeterminate dark matter by spiritual intent—here was the story to get to the ending—and that it was done by a process of discretion, the separation of day from night, air from water, earth from sky, one thing from another in, presumably, a six-day sequence culminating in the human race.

Every writer has to be awed by the staying power of the Genesis stories that have passed through the embellishing realms of oral transmission and the literate multilingual cultures of thousands of years. They are a group effort but not at all afflicted with the bureaucratic monotone that would be expected to characterize written collaborations. One reason for this may be the wisdom of the later scribes in leaving intact on the page those chronicles they felt obligated to improve upon. As a result we get more than one point of view, which has the effect, in the depiction of human character, of a given roundness or ambiguity that we recognize as realistic. Consider Jacob for example, who will wrestle with God or His representative and be named Israel, after all, but is impelled twice in his life to acts of gross deception—of his brother, Esau, and of his father, Isaac. Or the lovely gentle Rebecca, who as a maid displays the innocent generosity that the servant of Abraham seeks, offering him the water from her water jar, and then seeing to his camels . . . but years later, as the mother of Jacob, shrewishly assists her son in depriving Esau of his rightful patrimony.

In general, family life does not go all that smoothly for the founding generations. Beginning with Cain and Abel and persisting to the time of Joseph, brothers seem—like the brothers in fairy tales—to be seriously lacking in the fraternal spirit. Wives who are not themselves sufficiently fertile foist slave women on their husbands for purposes of impregnation, and then become jealous of those women and have them sent away. There seem to be two stations of wife, high and low—Hagar and Leah being examples of the low—and the anger and resentment this creates is palpable. Overall, the women of Genesis may be subject to an exclusively biological destiny as childbearers—theirs is a nomadic society that to survive must be fruitful—and the movable tent kingdoms in which they live may be unquestioningly paternalistic, but the modern reader cannot help but notice with relief how much grumbling they do.

It is in the pages of Genesis that the first two of the three major covenants between God and humanity are described. After the Flood, God assures Noah that He will not again lay waste to all creation in a flood. The sign of this covenant will be a rainbow in the clouds. Later, Abraham is commanded by God to resettle in Canaan, where he will be assured that he will eventually prevail as the father of many nations. Circumcision is the way Abraham and his descendants are to give sign of keeping this covenant. It is only in the next book, Exodus, that the final element of the covenantal religion, the Ten Commandments, will be given through Moses to his people. It is here that God will be identified as Yahweh and a ritualized sabbath—a simulation of God's day of rest after the Creation—is to be identified as the sign.

Apart from their religious profundity, this graduated series of exchanges between God and man have to remind us of the struggle for human distinction or identity in a precarious, brute life. This was the Bronze Age, after all. The Abrahamic generations were desert nomads, outlanders, who lived in tents while people such as the Egyptians lived in cities that were the heart of civilization. The territory that Abraham and his descendants were called to was abuzz with Amorites and other tribes of ethnically diverse Canaanites. Under such difficult circumstances it is understandable that the Abrahamic nomads' desire to be a designated people living in a state of moral consequence would direct them to bond with one God rather than many gods, and to find their solace and their courage in His singularity, His totality. But that they did so was tantamount to genius—and a considerable advance in the moral career of the human race.

For finally, as to literary strategies, it is the invention of character that is most telling, and in the Genesis narratives it is God Himself who is the most complex and riveting character. He seems at times to be as troubled and conflicted, as moved by the range of human feelings, as the human beings He has created. The personality of God cannot be an entirely unwitting set of traits in a theological text that declares that we are made in His image, after His likeness. There is an unmistakable implication of codependence. And it is no doubt some of the incentive for the idea expressed by the late Rabbi Abraham Joshua Heschel that the immanence of God, His existence in us, is manifest in the goodness of human works, the *mitzvot* or good deeds that reflect His nature. "Reverence," says the rabbi, "is the discovery of the world as an allusion to God." And so in reverence and ethical action do our troubled, conflicted minds find holiness, or bring it into being. Recognizing the glory of God is presumably our redemption, and our redemption is, presumably, His.

the first book of moses, called genesis

In the beginning God created the heaven and the earth. ²And the earth was without form, and void; and darkness was upon the face of the deep. And the Spirit of God moved upon the face of the waters. ³And God said, 'Let there be light': and there was light. ⁴And God saw the light, that it was good; and God divided the light from the darkness. ⁵And God called the light Day, and the darkness he called Night. And the evening and the morning were the first day.

⁶And God said, 'Let there be a firmament in the midst of the waters, and let it divide the waters from the waters.' ⁷And God made the firmament, and divided the waters which were under the firmament from the waters which were above the firmament; and it was so. ⁸And God called the firmament Heaven. And the evening and the morning were the second day.

⁹And God said, 'Let the waters under the heaven be gathered together unto one place, and let the dry land appear,' and it was so. ¹⁰And God called the dry land Earth; and the gathering together of the waters called he Seas; and God saw that it was good. ¹¹And God said, 'Let the earth bring forth grass, the herb yielding seed, and the fruit tree yielding fruit after his kind, whose seed is in itself, upon the earth,' and it

was so. [12]And the earth brought forth grass, and herb yielding seed after his kind, and the tree yielding fruit, whose seed was in itself, after his kind; and God saw that it was good. [13]And the evening and the morning were the third day.

[14]And God said, 'Let there be lights in the firmament of the heaven to divide the day from the night; and let them be for signs, and for seasons, and for days, and years; [15]and let them be for lights in the firmament of the heaven to give light upon the earth,' and it was so. [16]And God made two great lights: the greater light to rule the day, and the lesser light to rule the night; he made the stars also. [17]And God set them in the firmament of the heaven to give light upon the earth, [18]and to rule over the day and over the night, and to divide the light from the darkness; and God saw that it was good. [19]And the evening and the morning were the fourth day. [20]And God said, 'Let the waters bring forth abundantly the moving creature that hath life, and fowl that may fly above the earth in the open firmament of heaven.' [21]And God created great whales, and every living creature that moveth, which the waters brought forth abundantly, after their kind, and every winged fowl after his kind; and God saw that it was good. [22]And God blessed them, saying, 'Be fruitful, and multiply, and fill the waters in the seas, and let fowl multiply in the earth.' [23]And the evening and the morning were the fifth day.

[24]And God said, 'Let the earth bring forth the living creature after his kind, cattle, and creeping thing, and beast of the earth after his kind,' and it was so. [25]And God made the beast of the earth after his kind, and cattle after their kind,

and every thing that creepeth upon the earth after his kind: and God saw that it was good.

²⁶And God said, 'Let us make man in our image, after our likeness: and let them have dominion over the fish of the sea, and over the fowl of the air, and over the cattle, and over all the earth, and over every creeping thing that creepeth upon the earth.' ²⁷So God created man in his own image, in the image of God created he him; male and female created he them. ²⁸And God blessed them, and God said unto them, 'Be fruitful, and multiply, and replenish the earth, and subdue it: and have dominion over the fish of the sea, and over the fowl of the air, and over every living thing that moveth upon the earth.'

²⁹And God said, 'Behold, I have given you every herb bearing seed, which is upon the face of all the earth, and every tree, in the which is the fruit of a tree yielding seed; to you it shall be for meat. ³⁰And to every beast of the earth, and to every fowl of the air, and to every thing that creepeth upon the earth, wherein there is life, I have given every green herb for meat,' and it was so. ³¹And God saw every thing that he had made, and, behold, it was very good. And the evening and the morning were the sixth day.

2 Thus the heavens and the earth were finished, and all the host of them. ²And on the seventh day God ended his work which he had made; and he rested on the seventh day from all his work which he had made. ³And God blessed the seventh day, and sanctified it; because that in it he had

rested from all his work which God created and made.

⁴These are the generations of the heavens and of the earth when they were created, in the day that the Lord God made the earth and the heavens, ⁵and every plant of the field before it was in the earth, and every herb of the field before it grew; for the Lord God had not caused it to rain upon the earth, and there was not a man to till the ground. ⁶But there went up a mist from the earth, and watered the whole face of the ground. ⁷And the Lord God formed man of the dust of the ground, and breathed into his nostrils the breath of life; and man became a living soul.

⁸And the Lord God planted a garden eastward in Eden; and there he put the man whom he had formed. ⁹And out of the ground made the Lord God to grow every tree that is pleasant to the sight, and good for food; the tree of life also in the midst of the garden, and the tree of knowledge of good and evil. ¹⁰And a river went out of Eden to water the garden; and from thence it was parted, and became into four heads. ¹¹The name of the first is Pison: that is it which compasseth the whole land of Havilah, where there is gold; ¹²and the gold of that land is good; there is bdellium and the onyx stone. ¹³And the name of the second river is Gihon: the same is it that compasseth the whole land of Ethiopia. ¹⁴And the name of the third river is Hiddekel: that is it which goeth toward the east of Assyria. And the fourth river is Euphrates. ¹⁵And the Lord God took the man, and put him into the garden of Eden to dress it and to keep it. ¹⁶And the Lord God commanded the man, saying, 'Of every tree of the garden

thou mayest freely eat; ¹⁷ but of the tree of the knowledge of good and evil, thou shalt not eat of it; for in the day that thou eatest thereof thou shalt surely die.'

¹⁸And the Lord God said, 'It is not good that the man should be alone; I will make him an help meet for him.' ¹⁹And out of the ground the Lord God formed every beast of the field, and every fowl of the air; and brought them unto Adam to see what he would call them; and whatsoever Adam called every living creature, that was the name thereof. ²⁰And Adam gave names to all cattle, and to the fowl of the air, and to every beast of the field; but for Adam there was not found an help meet for him. ²¹And the Lord God caused a deep sleep to fall upon Adam, and he slept: and he took one of his ribs, and closed up the flesh instead thereof; ²² and the rib, which the Lord God had taken from man, made he a woman, and brought her unto the man. ²³And Adam said, 'This is now bone of my bones, and flesh of my flesh; she shall be called Woman, because she was taken out of Man.' ²⁴Therefore shall a man leave his father and his mother, and shall cleave unto his wife; and they shall be one flesh. ²⁵And they were both naked, the man and his wife, and were not ashamed.

3 Now the serpent was more subtil than any beast of the field which the Lord God had made. And he said unto the woman, 'Yea, hath God said, "Ye shall not eat of every tree of the garden"?' ²And the woman said unto the serpent, 'We may eat of the fruit of the trees of the garden; ³ but of the

fruit of the tree which is in the midst of the garden, God hath said, "Ye shall not eat of it, neither shall ye touch it, lest ye die."' ⁴And the serpent said unto the woman, 'Ye shall not surely die; ⁵for God doth know that in the day ye eat thereof, then your eyes shall be opened, and ye shall be as gods, knowing good and evil.' ⁶And when the woman saw that the tree was good for food, and that it was pleasant to the eyes, and a tree to be desired to make one wise, she took of the fruit thereof, and did eat, and gave also unto her husband with her; and he did eat. ⁷And the eyes of them both were opened, and they knew that they were naked; and they sewed fig leaves together, and made themselves aprons.

⁸And they heard the voice of the Lord God walking in the garden in the cool of the day; and Adam and his wife hid themselves from the presence of the Lord God amongst the trees of the garden. ⁹And the Lord God called unto Adam, and said unto him, 'Where art thou?' ¹⁰And he said, 'I heard thy voice in the garden, and I was afraid, because I was naked; and I hid myself.' ¹¹And he said, 'Who told thee that thou wast naked? Hast thou eaten of the tree, whereof I commanded thee that thou shouldest not eat?' ¹²And the man said, 'The woman whom thou gavest to be with me, she gave me of the tree, and I did eat.' ¹³And the Lord God said unto the woman, 'What is this that thou hast done?' And the woman said, 'The serpent beguiled me, and I did eat.' ¹⁴And the Lord God said unto the serpent, 'Because thou hast done this, thou art cursed above all cattle, and above every beast of the field; upon thy belly shalt thou go, and dust shalt thou

eat all the days of thy life. ¹⁵And I will put enmity between thee and the woman, and between thy seed and her seed; it shall bruise thy head, and thou shalt bruise his heel.' ¹⁶Unto the woman he said, 'I will greatly multiply thy sorrow and thy conception; in sorrow thou shalt bring forth children; and thy desire shall be to thy husband, and he shall rule over thee.' ¹⁷And unto Adam he said, 'Because thou hast hearkened unto the voice of thy wife, and hast eaten of the tree, of which I commanded thee, saying, "Thou shalt not eat of it": cursed is the ground for thy sake; in sorrow shalt thou eat of it all the days of thy life; ¹⁸thorns also and thistles shall it bring forth to thee; and thou shalt eat the herb of the field; ¹⁹in the sweat of thy face shalt thou eat bread, till thou return unto the ground; for out of it wast thou taken; for dust thou art, and unto dust shalt thou return.' ²⁰And Adam called his wife's name Eve; because she was the mother of all living. ²¹Unto Adam also and to his wife did the Lord God make coats of skins, and clothed them.

²²And the Lord God said, 'Behold, the man is become as one of us, to know good and evil; and now, lest he put forth his hand, and take also of the tree of life, and eat, and live for ever.' ²³Therefore the Lord God sent him forth from the garden of Eden, to till the ground from whence he was taken. ²⁴So he drove out the man; and he placed at the east of the garden of Eden Cherubims, and a flaming sword which turned every way, to keep the way of the tree of life.

4 And Adam knew Eve his wife; and she conceived, and bare Cain, and said, 'I have gotten a man from the Lord.' ²And she again bare his brother Abel. And Abel was a keeper of sheep, but Cain was a tiller of the ground. ³And in process of time it came to pass that Cain brought of the fruit of the ground an offering unto the Lord. ⁴And Abel, he also brought of the firstlings of his flock and of the fat thereof. And the Lord had respect unto Abel and to his offering; ⁵but unto Cain and to his offering he had not respect. And Cain was very wroth, and his countenance fell. ⁶And the Lord said unto Cain, 'Why art thou wroth? And why is thy countenance fallen? ⁷If thou doest well, shalt thou not be accepted? And if thou doest not well, sin lieth at the door. And unto thee shall be his desire, and thou shalt rule over him.' ⁸And Cain talked with Abel his brother; and it came to pass, when they were in the field, that Cain rose up against Abel his brother, and slew him.

⁹And the Lord said unto Cain, 'Where is Abel thy brother?' And he said, 'I know not. Am I my brother's keeper?' ¹⁰And he said, 'What hast thou done? The voice of thy brother's blood crieth unto me from the ground. ¹¹And now art thou cursed from the earth, which hath opened her mouth to receive thy brother's blood from thy hand; ¹²when thou tillest the ground, it shall not henceforth yield unto thee her strength; a fugitive and a vagabond shalt thou be in the earth.' ¹³And Cain said unto the Lord, 'My punishment is greater than I can bear. ¹⁴Behold, thou hast driven me out this day from the face of the earth; and from thy face shall I be hid;

and I shall be a fugitive and a vagabond in the earth; and it shall come to pass, that every one that findeth me shall slay me.' ¹⁵And the Lord said unto him, 'Therefore whosoever slayeth Cain, vengeance shall be taken on him sevenfold.' And the Lord set a mark upon Cain, lest any finding him should kill him.

¹⁶And Cain went out from the presence of the Lord, and dwelt in the land of Nod, on the east of Eden. ¹⁷And Cain knew his wife; and she conceived, and bare Enoch; and he builded a city, and called the name of the city, after the name of his son, Enoch. ¹⁸And unto Enoch was born Irad; and Irad begat Mehujael; and Mehujael begat Methusael; and Methusael begat Lamech.

¹⁹And Lamech took unto him two wives: the name of the one was Adah, and the name of the other Zillah. ²⁰And Adah bare Jabal; he was the father of such as dwell in tents, and of such as have cattle. ²¹And his brother's name was Jubal: he was the father of all such as handle the harp and organ. ²²And Zillah, she also bare Tubalcain, an instructer of every artificer in brass and iron; and the sister of Tubalcain was Naamah. ²³And Lamech said unto his wives, Adah and Zillah, 'Hear my voice; ye wives of Lamech, hearken unto my speech; for I have slain a man to my wounding, and a young man to my hurt. ²⁴If Cain shall be avenged sevenfold, truly Lamech seventy and sevenfold.'

²⁵And Adam knew his wife again; and she bare a son, and called his name Seth; 'For God,' said she, 'hath appointed me another seed instead of Abel, whom Cain slew.' ²⁶And to Seth,

to him also there was born a son; and he called his name Enos; then began men to call upon the name of the Lord.

5 This is the book of the generations of Adam. In the day that God created man, in the likeness of God made he him; ²male and female created he them; and blessed them, and called their name Adam, in the day when they were created.

³And Adam lived an hundred and thirty years, and begat a son in his own likeness, after his image; and called his name Seth; ⁴and the days of Adam after he had begotten Seth were eight hundred years; and he begat sons and daughters; ⁵and all the days that Adam lived were nine hundred and thirty years; and he died. ⁶And Seth lived an hundred and five years, and begat Enos; ⁷and Seth lived after he begat Enos eight hundred and seven years, and begat sons and daughters; ⁸and all the days of Seth were nine hundred and twelve years; and he died.

⁹And Enos lived ninety years, and begat Cainan; ¹⁰and Enos lived after he begat Cainan eight hundred and fifteen years, and begat sons and daughters; ¹¹and all the days of Enos were nine hundred and five years; and he died.

¹²And Cainan lived seventy years, and begat Mahalaleel; ¹³and Cainan lived after he begat Mahalaleel eight hundred and forty years, and begat sons and daughters; ¹⁴and all the days of Cainan were nine hundred and ten years; and he died.

¹⁵And Mahalaleel lived sixty and five years, and begat Jared; ¹⁶and Mahalaleel lived after he begat Jared eight hundred and thirty years, and begat sons and daughters; ¹⁷and

all the days of Mahalaleel were eight hundred ninety and five years; and he died.

¹⁸And Jared lived an hundred sixty and two years, and he begat Enoch; ¹⁹and Jared lived after he begat Enoch eight hundred years, and begat sons and daughters; ²⁰and all the days of Jared were nine hundred sixty and two years; and he died.

²¹And Enoch lived sixty and five years, and begat Methuselah; ²²and Enoch walked with God after he begat Methuselah three hundred years, and begat sons and daughters; ²³and all the days of Enoch were three hundred sixty and five years; ²⁴and Enoch walked with God; and he was not; for God took him. ²⁵And Methuselah lived an hundred eighty and seven years, and begat Lamech; ²⁶and Methuselah lived after he begat Lamech seven hundred eighty and two years, and begat sons and daughters; ²⁷and all the days of Methuselah were nine hundred sixty and nine years; and he died.

²⁸And Lamech lived an hundred eighty and two years, and begat a son; ²⁹and he called his name Noah, saying, 'This same shall comfort us concerning our work and toil of our hands, because of the ground which the Lord hath cursed.' ³⁰And Lamech lived after he begat Noah five hundred ninety and five years, and begat sons and daughters; ³¹and all the days of Lamech were seven hundred seventy and seven years; and he died. ³²And Noah was five hundred years old; and Noah begat Shem, Ham, and Japheth.

6 And it came to pass, when men began to multiply on the face of the earth, and daughters were born unto

them, ² that the sons of God saw the daughters of men that they were fair; and they took them wives of all which they chose. ³And the Lord said, 'My spirit shall not always strive with man, for that he also is flesh; yet his days shall be an hundred and twenty years.' ⁴There were giants in the earth in those days; and also after that, when the sons of God came in unto the daughters of men, and they bare children to them, the same became mighty men which were of old, men of renown.

⁵And God saw that the wickedness of man was great in the earth, and that every imagination of the thoughts of his heart was only evil continually. ⁶And it repented the Lord that he had made man on the earth, and it grieved him at his heart. ⁷And the Lord said, 'I will destroy man whom I have created from the face of the earth; both man, and beast, and the creeping thing, and the fowls of the air; for it repenteth me that I have made them.' ⁸But Noah found grace in the eyes of the Lord.

⁹There are the generations of Noah: Noah was a just man and perfect in his generations, and Noah walked with God. ¹⁰And Noah begat three sons, Shem, Ham, and Japheth. ¹¹The earth also was corrupt before God, and the earth was filled with violence. ¹²And God looked upon the earth, and, behold, it was corrupt; for all flesh had corrupted his way upon the earth. ¹³And God said unto Noah, 'The end of all flesh is come before me; for the earth is filled with violence through them; and, behold, I will destroy them with the earth.

¹⁴ 'Make thee an ark of gopher wood; rooms shalt thou

make in the ark, and shalt pitch it within and without with pitch. ¹⁵And this is the fashion which thou shalt make it of: the length of the ark shall be three hundred cubits, the breadth of it fifty cubits, and the height of it thirty cubits. ¹⁶A window shalt thou make to the ark, and in a cubit shalt thou finish it above; and the door of the ark shalt thou set in the side thereof; with lower, second, and third stories shalt thou make it. ¹⁷And, behold, I, even I, do bring a flood of waters upon the earth, to destroy all flesh, wherein is the breath of life, from under heaven; and every thing that is in the earth shall die. ¹⁸But with thee will I establish my covenant; and thou shalt come into the ark, thou, and thy sons, and thy wife, and thy sons' wives with thee. ¹⁹And of every living thing of all flesh, two of every sort shalt thou bring into the ark, to keep them alive with thee; they shall be male and female. ²⁰Of fowls after their kind, and of cattle after their kind, of every creeping thing of the earth after his kind, two of every sort shall come unto thee, to keep them alive. ²¹And take thou unto thee of all food that is eaten, and thou shalt gather it to thee; and it shall be for food for thee, and for them.' ²²Thus did Noah; according to all that God commanded him, so did he.

7 And the Lord said unto Noah, 'Come thou and all thy house into the ark; for thee have I seen righteous before me in this generation. ²Of every clean beast thou shalt take to thee by sevens, the male and his female; and of beasts that are not clean by two, the male and his female. ³Of fowls also

of the air by sevens, the male and the female; to keep seed alive upon the face of all the earth. ⁴ For yet seven days, and I will cause it to rain upon the earth forty days and forty nights; and every living substance that I have made will I destroy from off the face of the earth.' ⁵And Noah did according unto all that the Lord commanded him. ⁶And Noah was six hundred years old when the flood of waters was upon the earth.

⁷And Noah went in, and his sons, and his wife, and his sons' wives with him, into the ark, because of the waters of the flood. ⁸ Of clean beasts, and of beasts that are not clean, and of fowls, and of every thing that creepeth upon the earth, ⁹ there went in two and two unto Noah into the ark, the male and the female, as God had commanded Noah. ¹⁰And it came to pass after seven days, that the waters of the flood were upon the earth.

¹¹ In the six hundredth year of Noah's life, in the second month, the seventeenth day of the month, the same day were all the fountains of the great deep broken up, and the windows of heaven were opened. ¹²And the rain was upon the earth forty days and forty nights. ¹³ In the selfsame day entered Noah, and Shem, and Ham, and Japheth, the sons of Noah, and Noah's wife, and the three wives of his sons with them, into the ark; ¹⁴ they, and every beast after his kind, and all the cattle after their kind, and every creeping thing that creepeth upon the earth after his kind, and every fowl after his kind, every bird of every sort. ¹⁵And they went in unto Noah into the ark, two and two of all flesh, wherein is the breath of life. ¹⁶And they that went in, went in male and female of all flesh,

as God had commanded him: and the Lord shut him in. [17]And the flood was forty days upon the earth; and the waters increased, and bare up the ark, and it was lift up above the earth. [18]And the waters prevailed, and were increased greatly upon the earth; and the ark went upon the face of the waters. [19]And the waters prevailed exceedingly upon the earth; and all the high hills, that were under the whole heaven, were covered. [20]Fifteen cubits upward did the waters prevail; and the mountains were covered. [21]And all flesh died that moved upon the earth, both of fowl, and of cattle, and of beast, and of every creeping thing that creepeth upon the earth, and every man; [22]all in whose nostrils was the breath of life, of all that was in the dry land, died. [23]And every living substance was destroyed which was upon the face of the ground, both man, and cattle, and the creeping things, and the fowl of the heaven; and they were destroyed from the earth: and Noah only remained alive, and they that were with him in the ark. [24]And the waters prevailed upon the earth an hundred and fifty days.

8 And God remembered Noah, and every living thing, and all the cattle that was with him in the ark: and God made a wind to pass over the earth, and the waters asswaged; [2]the fountains also of the deep and the windows of heaven were stopped, and the rain from heaven was restrained; [3]and the waters returned from off the earth continually: and after the end of the hundred and fifty days the waters were abated. [4]And the ark rested in the seventh month, on the seventeenth day of the month, upon the mountains of Ararat. [5]And the

waters decreased continually until the tenth month; in the tenth month, on the first day of the month, were the tops of the mountains seen.

⁶And it came to pass at the end of forty days that Noah opened the window of the ark which he had made; ⁷and he sent forth a raven, which went forth to and fro, until the waters were dried up from off the earth. ⁸Also he sent forth a dove from him, to see if the waters were abated from off the face of the ground; ⁹but the dove found no rest for the sole of her foot, and she returned unto him into the ark, for the waters were on the face of the whole earth; then he put forth his hand, and took her, and pulled her in unto him into the ark. ¹⁰And he stayed yet other seven days; and again he sent forth the dove out of the ark; ¹¹and the dove came in to him in the evening; and, lo, in her mouth was an olive leaf pluckt off; so Noah knew that the waters were abated from off the earth. ¹²And he stayed yet other seven days; and sent forth the dove; which returned not again unto him any more.

¹³And it came to pass in the six hundredth and first year, in the first month, the first day of the month, the waters were dried up from off the earth; and Noah removed the covering of the ark, and looked, and, behold, the face of the ground was dry. ¹⁴And in the second month, on the seven and twentieth day of the month, was the earth dried.

¹⁵And God spake unto Noah, saying, ¹⁶'Go forth of the ark, thou, and thy wife, and thy sons, and thy sons' wives with thee. ¹⁷Bring forth with thee every living thing that is with thee, of all flesh, both of fowl, and of cattle, and of every

creeping thing that creepeth upon the earth; that they may breed abundantly in the earth, and be fruitful, and multiply upon the earth.' ¹⁸And Noah went forth, and his sons, and his wife, and his sons' wives with him; ¹⁹every beast, every creeping thing, and every fowl, and whatsoever creepeth upon the earth, after their kinds, went forth out of the ark.

²⁰And Noah builded an altar unto the Lord; and took of every clean beast, and of every clean fowl, and offered burnt offerings on the altar. ²¹And the Lord smelled a sweet savour; and the Lord said in his heart, 'I will not again curse the ground any more for man's sake; for the imagination of man's heart is evil from his youth; neither will I again smite any more every thing living, as I have done. ²²While the earth remaineth, seed-time and harvest, and cold and heat, and summer and winter, and day and night shall not cease.'

9 And God blessed Noah and his sons, and said unto them, 'Be fruitful, and multiply, and replenish the earth. ²And the fear of you and the dread of you shall be upon every beast of the earth, and upon every fowl of the air, upon all that moveth upon the earth, and upon all the fishes of the sea; into your hand are they delivered. ³Every moving thing that liveth shall be meat for you; even as the green herb have I given you all things. ⁴But flesh with the life thereof, which is the blood thereof, shall ye not eat. ⁵And surely your blood of your lives will I require; at the hand of every beast will I require it, and at the hand of man; at the hand of every man's brother will I require the life of man. ⁶Whoso sheddeth man's

blood, by man shall his blood be shed: for in the image of God made he man. ⁷And you, be ye fruitful, and multiply; bring forth abundantly in the earth, and multiply therein.'

⁸And God spake unto Noah, and to his sons with him, saying, ⁹'And I, behold, I establish my covenant with you, and with your seed after you; ¹⁰and with every living creature that is with you, of the fowl, of the cattle, and of every beast of the earth with you; from all that go out of the ark, to every beast of the earth. ¹¹And I will establish my covenant with you; neither shall all flesh be cut off any more by the waters of a flood; neither shall there any more be a flood to destroy the earth.'

¹²And God said, 'This is the token of the covenant which I make between me and you and every living creature that is with you, for perpetual generations: ¹³I do set my bow in the cloud, and it shall be for a token of a covenant between me and the earth. ¹⁴And it shall come to pass, when I bring a cloud over the earth, that the bow shall be seen in the cloud: ¹⁵and I will remember my covenant, which is between me and you and every living creature of all flesh; and the waters shall no more become a flood to destroy all flesh. ¹⁶And the bow shall be in the cloud; and I will look upon it, that I may remember the everlasting covenant between God and every living creature of all flesh that is upon the earth.' ¹⁷And God said unto Noah, 'This is the token of the covenant, which I have established between me and all flesh that is upon the earth.'

¹⁸And the sons of Noah, that went forth of the ark, were Shem, and Ham, and Japheth; and Ham is the father of Canaan. ¹⁹These are the three sons of Noah; and of them was the

whole earth overspread. ²⁰And Noah began to be an husbandman, and he planted a vineyard; ²¹and he drank of the wine, and was drunken; and he was uncovered within his tent. ²²And Ham, the father of Canaan, saw the nakedness of his father, and told his two brethren without. ²³And Shem and Japheth took a garment, and laid it upon both their shoulders, and went backward, and covered the nakedness of their father; and their faces were backward, and they saw not their father's nakedness. ²⁴And Noah awoke from his wine, and knew what his younger son had done unto him. ²⁵And he said, 'Cursed be Canaan; a servant of servants shall he be unto his brethren.' ²⁶And he said, 'Blessed be the Lord God of Shem; and Canaan shall be his servant. ²⁷God shall enlarge Japheth, and he shall dwell in the tents of Shem; and Canaan shall be his servant.'

²⁸And Noah lived after the flood three hundred and fifty years. ²⁹And all the days of Noah were nine hundred and fifty years: and he died.

10 Now these are the generations of the sons of Noah, Shem, Ham, and Japheth: and unto them were sons born after the flood. ²The sons of Japheth: Gomer, and Magog, and Madai, and Javan, and Tubal, and Meshech, and Tiras. ³And the sons of Gomer: Ashkenaz, and Riphath, and Togarmah. ⁴And the sons of Javan: Elishah, and Tarshish, Kittim, and Dodanim. ⁵By these were the isles of the Gentiles divided in their lands; every one after his tongue, after their families, in their nations.

⁶And the sons of Ham: Cush, and Mizraim, and Phut, and Canaan. ⁷And the sons of Cush: Seba, and Havilah, and Sabtah, and Raamah, and Sabtecha; and the sons of Raamah: Sheba, and Dedan. ⁸And Cush begat Nimrod; he began to be a mighty one in the earth. ⁹He was a mighty hunter before the Lord: wherefore it is said, 'Even as Nimrod the mighty hunter before the Lord.' ¹⁰And the beginning of his kingdom was Babel, and Erech, and Accad, and Calneh, in the land of Shinar. ¹¹Out of that land went forth Asshur, and builded Nineveh, and the city Rehoboth, and Calah, ¹²and Resen between Nineveh and Calah: the same is a great city. ¹³And Mizraim begat Ludim, and Anamim, and Lehabim, and Naphtuhim, ¹⁴and Pathrusim, and Casluhim (out of whom came Philistim) and Caphtorim.

¹⁵And Canaan begat Sidon his firstborn, and Heth, ¹⁶and the Jebusite, and the Amorite, and the Girgasite, ¹⁷and the Hivite, and the Arkite, and the Sinite, ¹⁸and the Arvadite, and the Zemarite, and the Hamathite: and afterward were the families of the Canaanites spread abroad. ¹⁹And the border of the Canaanites was from Sidon, as thou comest to Gerar, unto Gaza; as thou goest, unto Sodom, and Gomorrah, and Admah, and Zeboim, even unto Lasha. ²⁰These are the sons of Ham, after their families, after their tongues, in their countries, and in their nations.

²¹Unto Shem also, the father of all the children of Eber, the brother of Japheth the elder, even to him were children born. ²²The children of Shem: Elam, and Asshur, and Arphaxad, and Lud, and Aram. ²³And the children of Aram: Uz,

and Hul, and Gether, and Mash. 24And Arphaxad begat Salah; and Salah begat Eber. 25And unto Eber were born two sons: the name of one was Peleg; for in his days was the earth divided; and his brother's name was Joktan. 26And Joktan begat Almodad, and Sheleph, and Hazarmaveth, and Jerah, 27and Hadoram, and Uzal, and Diklah, 28and Obal, and Abimael, and Sheba, 29and Ophir, and Havilah, and Jobab: all these were the sons of Joktan.30And their dwelling was from Mesha, as thou goest unto Sephar a mount of the east. 31These are the sons of Shem, after their families, after their tongues, in their lands, after their nations. 32These are the families of the sons of Noah, after their generations, in their nations: and by these were the nations divided in the earth after the flood.

11 And the whole earth was of one language, and of one speech. 2And it came to pass, as they journeyed from the east, that they found a plain in the land of Shinar; and they dwelt there. 3And they said one to another, 'Go to, let us make brick, and burn them throughly.' And they had brick for stone, and slime had they for morter. 4And they said, 'Go to, let us build us a city and a tower, whose top may reach unto heaven; and let us make us a name, lest we be scattered abroad upon the face of the whole earth.' 5And the Lord came down to see the city and the tower, which the children of men builded. 6And the Lord said, 'Behold, the people is one, and they have all one language; and this they begin to do; and now nothing will be restrained from them, which

they have imagined to do. ⁷Go to, let us go down, and there confound their language, that they may not understand one another's speech.' ⁸So the Lord scattered them abroad from thence upon the face of all the earth; and they left off to build the city. ⁹Therefore is the name of it called Babel; because the Lord did there confound the language of all the earth: and from thence did the Lord scatter them abroad upon the face of all the earth.

¹⁰These are the generations of Shem: Shem was an hundred years old, and begat Arphaxad two years after the flood; ¹¹and Shem lived after he begat Arphaxad five hundred years, and begat sons and daughters. ¹²And Arphaxad lived five and thirty years, and begat Salah; ¹³and Arphaxad lived after he begat Salah four hundred and three years, and begat sons and daughters.

¹⁴And Salah lived thirty years, and begat Eber; ¹⁵and Salah lived after he begat Eber four hundred and three years, and begat sons and daughters.

¹⁶And Eber lived four and thirty years, and begat Peleg; ¹⁷and Eber lived after he begat Peleg four hundred and thirty years, and begat sons and daughters.

¹⁸And Peleg lived thirty years, and begat Reu; ¹⁹and Peleg lived after he begat Reu two hundred and nine years, and begat sons and daughters.

²⁰And Reu lived two and thirty years, and begat Serug: ²¹and Reu lived after he begat Serug two hundred and seven years, and begat sons and daughters.

²²And Serug lived thirty years, and begat Nahor; ²³and

Serug lived after he begat Nahor two hundred years, and begat sons and daughters.

²⁴And Nahor lived nine and twenty years, and begat Terah; ²⁵and Nahor lived after he begat Terah an hundred and nineteen years, and begat sons and daughters.

²⁶And Terah lived seventy years, and begat Abram, Nahor, and Haran.

²⁷Now these are the generations of Terah: Terah begat Abram, Nahor, and Haran; and Haran begat Lot. ²⁸And Haran died before his father Terah in the land of his nativity, in Ur of the Chaldees. ²⁹And Abram and Nahor took them wives: the name of Abram's wife was Sarai; and the name of Nahor's wife, Milcah, the daughter of Haran, the father of Milcah, and the father of Iscah. ³⁰But Sarai was barren; she had no child. ³¹And Terah took Abram his son, and Lot the son of Haran his son's son, and Sarai his daughter in law, his son Abram's wife; and they went forth with them from Ur of the Chaldees, to go into the land of Canaan; and they came unto Haran, and dwelt there. ³²And the days of Terah were two hundred and five years; and Terah died in Haran.

12 Now the Lord had said unto Abram, 'Get thee out of thy country, and from thy kindred, and from thy father's house, unto a land that I will shew thee; ²and I will make of thee a great nation, and I will bless thee, and make thy name great; and thou shalt be a blessing; ³and I will bless them that bless thee, and curse him that curseth thee; and in thee shall all families of the earth be blessed.' ⁴So

Abram departed, as the Lord had spoken unto him; and Lot went with him: and Abram was seventy and five years old when he departed out of Haran. ⁵And Abram took Sarai his wife, and Lot his brother's son, and all their substance that they had gathered, and the souls that they had gotten in Haran; and they went forth to go into the land of Canaan; and into the land of Canaan they came.

⁶And Abram passed through the land unto the place of Sichem, unto the plain of Moreh. And the Canaanite was then in the land. ⁷And the Lord appeared unto Abram, and said, 'Unto thy seed will I give this land,' and there builded he an altar unto the Lord, who appeared unto him. ⁸And he removed from thence unto a mountain on the east of Beth-el, and pitched his tent, having Beth-el on the west, and Hai on the east; and there he builded an altar unto the Lord, and called upon the name of the Lord. ⁹And Abram journeyed, going on still toward the south.

¹⁰And there was a famine in the land; and Abram went down into Egypt to sojourn there; for the famine was grievous in the land. ¹¹And it came to pass, when he was come near to enter into Egypt, that he said unto Sarai his wife, 'Behold now, I know that thou art a fair woman to look upon. ¹² Therefore it shall come to pass, when the Egyptians shall see thee, that they shall say, "This is his wife," and they will kill me, but they will save thee alive. ¹³ Say, I pray thee, thou art my sister: that it may be well with me for thy sake; and my soul shall live because of thee.'

¹⁴And it came to pass, that, when Abram was come into

Egypt, the Egyptians beheld the woman that she was very fair. ¹⁵ The princes also of Pharaoh saw her, and commended her before Pharaoh: and the woman was taken into Pharaoh's house. ¹⁶And he entreated Abram well for her sake; and he had sheep, and oxen, and he asses, and menservants, and maidservants, and she asses, and camels. ¹⁷And the Lord plagued Pharaoh and his house with great plagues because of Sarai Abram's wife. ¹⁸And Pharaoh called Abram, and said, 'What is this that thou hast done unto me? Why didst thou not tell me that she was thy wife? ¹⁹ Why saidst thou, "She is my sister" so I might have taken her to me to wife? Now therefore behold thy wife, take her, and go thy way.' ²⁰And Pharaoh commanded his men concerning him: and they sent him away, and his wife, and all that he had.

13 And Abram went up out of Egypt, he, and his wife, and all that he had, and Lot with him, into the south. ²And Abram was very rich in cattle, in silver, and in gold. ³And he went on his journeys from the south even to Beth-el, unto the place where his tent had been at the beginning, between Beth-el and Hai; ⁴ unto the place of the altar, which he had made there at the first: and there Abram called on the name of the Lord.

⁵And Lot also, which went with Abram, had flocks, and herds, and tents. ⁶And the land was not able to bear them, that they might dwell together: for their substance was great, so that they could not dwell together. ⁷And there was a strife between the herdmen of Abram's cattle and the herdmen of

Lot's cattle; and the Canaanite and the Perizzite dwelled then in the land. ⁸And Abram said unto Lot, 'Let there be no strife, I pray thee, between me and thee, and between my herdmen and thy herdmen; for we be brethren. ⁹Is not the whole land before thee? Separate thyself, I pray thee, from me: if thou wilt take the left hand, then I will go to the right; or if thou depart to the right hand, then I will go to the left.' ¹⁰And Lot lifted up his eyes, and beheld all the plain of Jordan, that it was well watered every where, before the Lord destroyed Sodom and Gomorrah, even as the garden of the Lord, like the land of Egypt, as thcu comest unto Zoar. ¹¹Then Lot chose him all the plain of Jordan; and Lot journeyed east: and they separated themselves the one from the other. ¹²Abram dwelled in the land of Canaan, and Lot dwelled in the cities of the plain, and pitched his tent toward Sodom. ¹³ But the men of Sodom were wicked and sinners before the Lord exceedingly.

¹⁴And the Lord said unto Abram, after that Lot was separated from him, 'Lift up now thine eyes, and look from the place where thou art northward, and southward, and eastward, and westward: ¹⁵for all the land which thou seest, to thee will I give it, and to thy seed for ever. ¹⁶And I will make thy seed as the dust of the earth; so that if a man can number the dust of the earth, then shall thy seed also be numbered. ¹⁷Arise, walk through the land in the length of it and in the breadth of it; for I will give it unto thee.' ¹⁸Then Abram removed his tent, and came and dwelt in the plain of Mamre, which is in Hebron, and built there an altar unto the Lord.

14 And it came to pass in the days of Amraphel king of Shinar, Arioch king of Ellasar, Chedorlaomer king of Elam, and Tidal king of nations; ²that these made war with Bera king of Sodom, and with Birsha king of Gomorrah, Shinab king of Admah, and Shemeber king of Zeboiim, and the king of Bela, which is Zoar. ³All these were joined together in the vale of Siddim, which is the salt sea. ⁴Twelve years they served Chedorlaomer, and in the thirteenth year they rebelled. ⁵And in the fourteenth year came Chedorlaomer, and the kings that were with him, and smote the Rephaims in Ashteroth Karnaim, and the Zuzims in Ham, and the Emims in Shaveh Kiriathaim, ⁶and the Horites in their mount Seir, unto El-paran, which is by the wilderness. ⁷And they returned, and came to Enmishpat, which is Kadesh, and smote all the country of the Amalekites, and also the Amorites, that dwelt in Hazezontamar. ⁸And there went out the king of Sodom, and the king of Gomorrah, and the king of Admah, and the king of Zeboiim, and the king of Bela (the same is Zoar); and they joined battle with them in the vale of Siddim; ⁹with Chedorlaomer the king of Elam, and with Tidal king of nations, and Amraphel king of Shinar, and Arioch king of Ellasar; four kings with five. ¹⁰And the vale of Siddim was full of slimepits; and the kings of Sodom and Gomorrah fled, and fell there; and they that remained fled to the mountain. ¹¹And they took all the goods of Sodom and Gomorrah, and all their victuals, and went their way. ¹²And they took Lot, Abram's brother's son, who dwelt in Sodom, and his goods, and departed.

¹³And there came one that had escaped, and told Abram the Hebrew; for he dwelt in the plain of Mamre the Amorite, brother of Eshcol, and brother of Aner: and these were confederate with Abram. ¹⁴And when Abram heard that his brother was taken captive, he armed his trained servants, born in his own house, three hundred and eighteen, and pursued them unto Dan. ¹⁵And he divided himself against them, he and his servants, by night, and smote them, and pursued them unto Hobah, which is on the left hand of Damascus. ¹⁶And he brought back all the goods, and also brought again his brother Lot, and his goods, and the women also, and the people.

¹⁷And the king of Sodom went out to meet him after his return from the slaughter of Chedorlaomer, and of the kings that were with him, at the valley of Shaveh, which is the king's dale.

¹⁸And Melchizedek king of Salem brought forth bread and wine; and he was the priest of the most high God. ¹⁹And he blessed him, and said, 'Blessed be Abram of the most high God, possessor of heaven and earth; ²⁰and blessed be the most high God, which hath delivered thine enemies into thy hand.' And he gave him tithes of all. ²¹And the king of Sodom said unto Abram, 'Give me the persons, and take the goods to thyself.' ²²And Abram said to the king of Sodom, 'I have lift up mine hand unto the Lord, the most high God, the possessor of heaven and earth, ²³that I will not take from a thread even to a shoelatchet, and that I will not take any thing that is thine, lest thou shouldest say, "I have made Abram rich," ²⁴save only that which the young men have

eaten, and the portion of the men which went with me, Aner, Eshcol, and Mamre; let them take their portion.'

15 After these things the word of the Lord came unto Abram in a vision, saying, 'Fear not, Abram: I am thy shield, and thy exceeding great reward.' ²And Abram said, 'Lord God, what wilt thou give me, seeing I go childless, and the steward of my house is this Eliezer of Damascus?' ³And Abram said, 'Behold, to me thou hast given no seed; and, lo, one born in my house is mine heir.' ⁴And, behold, the word of the Lord came unto him, saying, 'This shall not be thine heir; but he that shall come forth out of thine own bowels shall be thine heir.' ⁵And he brought Abram forth abroad, and said, 'Look now toward heaven, and tell the stars, if thou be able to number them,' and he said unto him, 'So shall thy seed be.'

⁶And he believed in the Lord; and he counted it to him for righteousness. ⁷And he said unto him, 'I am the Lord that brought thee out of Ur of the Chaldees, to give thee this land to inherit it.' ⁸And he said, 'Lord God, whereby shall I know that I shall inherit it?' ⁹And the Lord said unto him, 'Take me an heifer of three years old, and a she goat of three years old, and a ram of three years old, and a turtledove, and a young pigeon.' ¹⁰And he took unto him all these, and divided them in the midst, and laid each piece one against another; but the birds divided he not. ¹¹And when the fowls came down upon the carcases, Abram drove them away. ¹²And when the sun was going down, a deep sleep fell upon Abram; and, lo, an

horror of great darkness fell upon him. ¹³And he said unto Abram, 'Know of a surety that thy seed shall be a stranger in a land that is not theirs, and shall serve them; and they shall afflict them four hundred years; ¹⁴and also that nation, whom they shall serve, will I judge: and afterward shall they come out with great substance. ¹⁵And thou shalt go to thy fathers in peace; thou shalt be buried in a good old age. ¹⁶But in the fourth generation they shall come hither again: for the iniquity of the Amorites is not yet full.' ¹⁷And it came to pass, that, when the sun went down, and it was dark, behold a smoking furnace, and a burning lamp that passed between those pieces. ¹⁸In the same day the Lord made a covenant with Abram, saying, 'Unto thy seed have I given this land, from the river of Egypt unto the great river, the river Euphrates: ¹⁹the Kenites, and the Kenizzites, and the Kadmonites, ²⁰and the Hittites, and the Perizzites, and the Rephaims, ²¹and the Amorites, and the Canaanites, and the Girgashites, and the Jebusites.'

16 Now Sarai Abram's wife bare him no children; and she had an handmaid, an Egyptian, whose name was Hagar. ²And Sarai said unto Abram, 'Behold now, the Lord hath restrained me from bearing; I pray thee, go in unto my maid; it may be that I may obtain children by her.' And Abram hearkened to the voice of Sarai. ³And Sarai Abram's wife took Hagar her maid the Egyptian, after Abram had dwelt ten years in the land of Canaan, and gave her to her husband Abram to be his wife.

⁴And he went in unto Hagar, and she conceived; and when

she saw that she had conceived, her mistress was despised in her eyes. ⁵And Sarai said unto Abram, 'My wrong be upon thee: I have given my maid into thy bosom; and when she saw that she had conceived, I was despised in her eyes; the Lord judge between me and thee.' ⁶But Abram said unto Sarai, 'Behold, thy maid is in thy hand; do to her as it pleaseth thee.' And when Sarai dealt hardly with her, she fled from her face.

⁷And the angel of the Lord found her by a fountain of water in the wilderness, by the fountain in the way to Shur. ⁸And he said, 'Hagar, Sarai's maid, whence camest thou? And whither wilt thou go?' And she said, 'I flee from the face of my mistress Sarai.' ⁹And the angel of the Lord said unto her, 'Return to thy mistress, and submit thyself under her hands.' ¹⁰And the angel of the Lord said unto her, 'I will multiply thy seed exceedingly, that it shall not be numbered for multitude.' ¹¹And the angel of the Lord said unto her, 'Behold, thou art with child, and shalt bear a son, and shalt call his name Ishmael; because the Lord hath heard thy affliction. ¹²And he will be a wild man; his hand will be against every man, and every man's hand against him; and he shall dwell in the presence of all his brethren.' ¹³And she called the name of the Lord that spake unto her, 'Thou God seest me,' for she said, 'Have I also here looked after him that seeth me?' ¹⁴Wherefore the well was called Beerlahai-roi; behold, it is between Kadesh and Bered.

¹⁵And Hagar bare Abram a son; and Abram called his son's name, which Hagar bare, Ishmael. ¹⁶And Abram was fourscore and six years old, when Hagar bare Ishmael to Abram.

17 And when Abram was ninety years old and nine, the Lord appeared to Abram, and said unto him, 'I am the Almighty God; walk before me, and be thou perfect. ²And I will make my covenant between me and thee, and will multiply thee exceedingly.' ³And Abram fell on his face: and God talked with him, saying, ⁴'As for me, behold, my covenant is with thee, and thou shalt be a father of many nations. ⁵Neither shall thy name any more be called Abram, but thy name shall be Abraham; for a father of many nations have I made thee. ⁶And I will make thee exceeding fruitful, and I will make nations of thee, and kings shall come out of thee. ⁷And I will establish my covenant between me and thee and thy seed after thee in their generations for an everlasting covenant, to be a God unto thee, and to thy seed after thee. ⁸And I will give unto thee, and to thy seed after thee, the land wherein thou art a stranger, all the land of Canaan, for an everlasting possession; and I will be their God.'

⁹And God said unto Abraham, 'Thou shalt keep my covenant therefore, thou, and thy seed after thee in their generations. ¹⁰This is my covenant, which ye shall keep, between me and you and thy seed after thee; every man child among you shall be circumcised. ¹¹And ye shall circumcise the flesh of your foreskin; and it shall be a token of the covenant betwixt me and you. ¹²And he that is eight days old shall be circumcised among you, every man child in your generations, he that is born in the house, or bought with money of any stranger, which is not of thy seed. ¹³He that is born in thy house, and he that is bought with thy money, must needs be circumcised;

and my covenant shall be in your flesh for an everlasting covenant. ¹⁴And the uncircumcised man child whose flesh of his foreskin is not circumcised, that soul shall be cut off from his people; he hath broken my covenant.'

¹⁵And God said unto Abraham, 'As for Sarai thy wife, thou shalt not call her name Sarai, but Sarah shall her name be. ¹⁶And I will bless her, and give thee a son also of her; yea, I will bless her, and she shall be a mother of nations; kings of people shall be of her.' ¹⁷Then Abraham fell upon his face, and laughed, and said in his heart, 'Shall a child be born unto him that is an hundred years old? And shall Sarah, that is ninety years old, bear?' ¹⁸And Abraham said unto God, 'O that Ishmael might live before thee!' ¹⁹And God said, 'Sarah thy wife shall bear thee a son indeed; and thou shalt call his name Isaac; and I will establish my covenant with him for an everlasting covenant, and with his seed after him. ²⁰And as for Ishmael, I have heard thee. Behold, I have blessed him, and will make him fruitful, and will multiply him exceedingly; twelve princes shall he beget, and I will make him a great nation. ²¹But my covenant will I establish with Isaac, which Sarah shall bear unto thee at this set time in the next year.' ²²And he left off talking with him, and God went up from Abraham.

²³And Abraham took Ishmael his son, and all that were born in his house, and all that were bought with his money, every male among the men of Abraham's house; and circumcised the flesh of their foreskin in the selfsame day, as God had said unto him. ²⁴And Abraham was ninety years old and nine, when he was circumcised in the flesh of his foreskin. ²⁵And

Ishmael his son was thirteen years old, when he was circumcised in the flesh of his foreskin. ²⁶ In the selfsame day was Abraham circumcised, and Ishmael his son. ²⁷ And all the men of his house, born in the house, and bought with money of the stranger, were circumcised with him.

18 And the Lord appeared unto him in the plains of Mamre; and he sat in the tent door in the heat of the day; ² and he lift up his eyes and looked, and, lo, three men stood by him: and when he saw them, he ran to meet them from the tent door, and bowed himself toward the ground, ³ and said, 'My Lord, if now I have found favour in thy sight, pass not away, I pray thee, from thy servant; ⁴ let a little water, I pray you, be fetched, and wash your feet, and rest yourselves under the tree; ⁵ and I will fetch a morsel of bread, and comfort ye your hearts; after that ye shall pass on; for therefore are ye come to your servant.' And they said, 'So do, as thou hast said.' ⁶ And Abraham hastened into the tent unto Sarah, and said, 'Make ready quickly three measures of fine meal, knead it, and make cakes upon the hearth.' ⁷ And Abraham ran unto the herd, and fetcht a calf tender and good, and gave it unto a young man; and he hasted to dress it. ⁸ And he took butter, and milk, and the calf which he had dressed, and set it before them; and he stood by them under the tree, and they did eat.

⁹ And they said unto him, 'Where is Sarah thy wife?' And he said, 'Behold, in the tent.' ¹⁰ And he said, 'I will certainly return unto thee according to the time of life; and, lo, Sarah

thy wife shall have a son.' And Sarah heard it in the tent door, which was behind him. [11]Now Abraham and Sarah were old and well stricken in age; and it ceased to be with Sarah after the manner of women. [12]Therefore Sarah laughed within herself, saying, 'After I am waxed old shall I have pleasure, my lord being old also?' [13]And the Lord said unto Abraham, 'Wherefore did Sarah laugh, saying, "Shall I of a surety bear a child, which am old?" [14]Is any thing too hard for the Lord? At the time appointed I will return unto thee, according to the time of life, and Sarah shall have a son.' [15]Then Sarah denied, saying, 'I laughed not', for she was afraid. And he said, 'Nay; but thou didst laugh.'

[16]And the men rose up from thence, and looked toward Sodom; and Abraham went with them to bring them on the way. [17]And the Lord said, 'Shall I hide from Abraham that thing which I do; [18]seeing that Abraham shall surely become a great and mighty nation, and all the nations of the earth shall be blessed in him? [19]For I know him, that he will command his children and his household after him, and they shall keep the way of the Lord, to do justice and judgment; that the Lord may bring upon Abraham that which he hath spoken of him.' [20]And the Lord said, 'Because the cry of Sodom and Gomorrah is great, and because their sin is very grievous; [21]I will go down now, and see whether they have done altogether according to the cry of it, which is come unto me; and if not, I will know.' [22]And the men turned their faces from thence, and went toward Sodom; but Abraham stood yet before the Lord.

²³And Abraham drew near, and said, 'Wilt thou also destroy the righteous with the wicked? ²⁴Peradventure there be fifty righteous within the city; wilt thou also destroy and not spare the place for the fifty righteous that are therein? ²⁵That be far from thee to do after this manner, to slay the righteous with the wicked: and that the righteous should be as the wicked, that be far from thee; shall not the Judge of all the earth do right?' ²⁶And the Lord said, 'If I find in Sodom fifty righteous within the city, then I will spare all the place for their sakes.' ²⁷And Abraham answered and said, 'Behold now, I have taken upon me to speak unto the Lord, which am but dust and ashes: ²⁸peradventure there shall lack five of the fifty righteous; wilt thou destroy all the city for lack of five?' And he said, 'If I find there forty and five, I will not destroy it.' ²⁹And he spake unto him yet again, and said, 'Peradventure there shall be forty found there.' And he said, 'I will not do it for forty's sake.' ³⁰And he said unto him, 'Oh let not the Lord be angry, and I will speak: peradventure there shall thirty be found there.' And he said, 'I will not do it, if I find thirty there.' ³¹And he said, 'Behold now, I have taken upon me to speak unto the Lord: peradventure there shall be twenty found there.' And he said, 'I will not destroy it for twenty's sake.' ³²And he said, 'Oh let not the Lord be angry, and I will speak yet but this once: peradventure ten shall be found there.' And he said, 'I will not destroy it for ten's sake.' ³³And the Lord went his way, as soon as he had left communing with Abraham; and Abraham returned unto his place.

19 And there came two angels to Sodom at even; and Lot sat in the gate of Sodom; and Lot seeing them rose up to meet them; and he bowed himself with his face toward the ground; ²and he said, 'Behold now, my lords, turn in, I pray you, into your servant's house, and tarry all night, and wash your feet, and ye shall rise up early, and go on your ways.' And they said, 'Nay; but we will abide in the street all night.' ³And he pressed upon them greatly; and they turned in unto him, and entered into his house; and he made them a feast, and did bake unleavened bread, and they did eat.

⁴But before they lay down, the men of the city, even the men of Sodom, compassed the house round, both old and young, all the people from every quarter; ⁵and they called unto Lot, and said unto him, 'Where are the men which came in to thee this night? Bring them out unto us, that we may know them.' ⁶And Lot went out at the door unto them, and shut the door after him, ⁷and said, 'I pray you, brethren, do not so wickedly. ⁸Behold now, I have two daughters which have not known man; let me, I pray you, bring them out unto you, and do ye to them as is good in your eyes: only unto these men do nothing; for therefore came they under the shadow of my roof.' ⁹And they said, 'Stand back.' And they said again, 'This one fellow came in to sojourn, and he will needs be a judge; now will we deal worse with thee, than with them.' And they pressed sore upon the man, even Lot, and came near to break the door. ¹⁰But the men put forth their hand, and pulled Lot into the house to them, and shut to the door. ¹¹And they smote the men that were at the door

of the house with blindness, both small and great; so that they wearied themselves to find the door.

¹²And the men said unto Lot, 'Hast thou here any besides? Son in law, and thy sons, and thy daughters, and whatsoever thou hast in the city, bring them out of this place, ¹³for we will destroy this place, because the cry of them is waxen great before the face of the Lord; and the Lord hath sent us to destroy it.' ¹⁴And Lot went out, and spake unto his sons in law, which married his daughters, and said, 'Up, get you out of this place; for the Lord will destroy this city.' But he seemed as one that mocked unto his sons in law.

¹⁵And when the morning arose, then the angels hastened Lot, saying, 'Arise, take thy wife, and thy two daughters, which are here; lest thou be consumed in the iniquity of the city.' ¹⁶And while he lingered, the men laid hold upon his hand, and upon the hand of his wife, and upon the hand of his two daughters; the Lord being merciful unto him; and they brought him forth, and set him without the city.

¹⁷And it came to pass, when they had brought them forth abroad, that he said, 'Escape for thy life; look not behind thee, neither stay thou in all the plain; escape to the mountain, lest thou be consumed.' ¹⁸And Lot said unto them, 'Oh, not so, my Lord: ¹⁹behold now, thy servant hath found grace in thy sight, and thou hast magnified thy mercy, which thou hast shewed unto me in saving my life; and I cannot escape to the mountain, lest some evil take me, and I die; ²⁰behold now, this city is near to flee unto, and it is a little one; oh, let me escape thither (is it not a little one?) and my soul shall

live.' ²¹And he said unto him, 'See, I have accepted thee concerning this thing also, that I will not overthrow this city, for the which thou hast spoken. ²²Haste thee, escape thither; for I cannot do any thing till thou be come thither.' Therefore the name of the city was called Zoar.

²³The sun was risen upon the earth when Lot entered into Zoar. ²⁴Then the Lord rained upon Sodom and upon Gomorrah brimstone and fire from the Lord out of heaven; ²⁵and he overthrew those cities, and all the plain, and all the inhabitants of the cities, and that which grew upon the ground.

²⁶But his wife looked back from behind him, and she became a pillar of salt.

²⁷And Abraham gat up early in the morning to the place where he stood before the Lord; ²⁸and he looked toward Sodom and Gomorrah, and toward all the land of the plain, and beheld, and, lo, the smoke of the country went up as the smoke of a furnace.

²⁹And it came to pass, when God destroyed the cities of the plain, that God remembered Abraham, and sent Lot out of the midst of the overthrow, when he overthrew the cities in the which Lot dwelt.

³⁰And Lot went up out of Zoar, and dwelt in the mountain, and his two daughters with him; for he feared to dwell in Zoar; and he dwelt in a cave, he and his two daughters. ³¹And the firstborn said unto the younger, 'Our father is old, and there is not a man in the earth to come in unto us after the manner of all the earth; ³²come, let us make our father drink wine, and we will lie with him, that we may preserve

seed of our father.' ³³And they made their father drink wine that night: and the firstborn went in, and lay with her father; and he perceived not when she lay down, nor when she arose. ³⁴And it came to pass on the morrow, that the firstborn said unto the younger, 'Behold, I lay yesternight with my father; let us make him drink wine this night also; and go thou in, and lie with him, that we may preserve seed of our father.' ³⁵And they made their father drink wine that night also; and the younger arose, and lay with him; and he perceived not when she lay down, nor when she arose. ³⁶Thus were both the daughters of Lot with child by their father. ³⁷And the firstborn bare a son, and called his name Moab; the same is the father of the Moabites unto this day. ³⁸And the younger, she also bare a son, and called his name Ben-ammi: the same is the father of the children of Ammon unto this day.

20 And Abraham journeyed from thence toward the south country, and dwelled between Kadesh and Shur, and sojourned in Gerar. ²And Abraham said of Sarah his wife, 'She is my sister,' and Abimelech king of Gerar sent, and took Sarah. ³But God came to Abimelech in a dream by night, and said to him, 'Behold, thou art but a dead man, for the woman which thou hast taken; for she is a man's wife.' ⁴But Abimelech had not come near her; and he said, 'Lord, wilt thou slay also a righteous nation? ⁵Said he not unto me, "She is my sister"? And she, even she herself said, "He is my brother"; in the integrity of my heart and innocency of my hands have I done this.' ⁶And God said unto him in a dream,

'Yea, I know that thou didst this in the integrity of thy heart; for I also withheld thee from sinning against me; therefore suffered I thee not to touch her. ⁷ Now therefore restore the man his wife; for he is a prophet, and he shall pray for thee, and thou shalt live; and if thou restore her not, know thou that thou shalt surely die, thou, and all that are thine.' ⁸ Therefore Abimelech rose early in the morning, and called all his servants, and told all these things in their ears; and the men were sore afraid. ⁹ Then Abimelech called Abraham, and said unto him, 'What hast thou done unto us? And what have I offended thee, that thou hast brought on me and on my kingdom a great sin? Thou hast done deeds unto me that ought not to be done.' ¹⁰ And Abimelech said unto Abraham, 'What sawest thou, that thou hast done this thing?' ¹¹ And Abraham said, 'Because I thought, surely the fear of God is not in this place; and they will slay me for my wife's sake. ¹² And yet indeed she is my sister; she is the daughter of my father, but not the daughter of my mother; and she became my wife. ¹³ And it came to pass, when God caused me to wander from my father's house, that I said unto her, "This is thy kindness which thou shalt shew unto me; at every place whither we shall come, say of me, 'He is my brother.'"' ¹⁴ And Abimelech took sheep, and oxen, and menservants, and womenservants, and gave them unto Abraham, and restored him Sarah his wife. ¹⁵ And Abimelech said, 'Behold, my land is before thee; dwell where it pleaseth thee.' ¹⁶ And unto Sarah he said, 'Behold, I have given thy brother a thousand pieces of silver; behold, he is to thee a covering of the eyes, unto all that are with thee, and with all other'; thus she was reproved.

¹⁷ So Abraham prayed unto God: and God healed Abimelech, and his wife, and his maidservants; and they bare children. ¹⁸ For the Lord had fast closed up all the wombs of the house of Abimelech, because of Sarah Abraham's wife.

21 And the Lord visited Sarah as he had said, and the Lord did unto Sarah as he had spoken. ² For Sarah conceived, and bare Abraham a son in his old age, at the set time of which God had spoken to him. ³ And Abraham called the name of his son that was born unto him, whom Sarah bare to him, Isaac. ⁴ And Abraham circumcised his son Isaac being eight days old, as God had commanded him. ⁵ And Abraham was an hundred years old, when his son Isaac was born unto him.

⁶ And Sarah said, 'God hath made me to laugh, so that all that hear will laugh with me.' ⁷ And she said, 'Who would have said unto Abraham, that Sarah should have given children suck? For I have born him a son in his old age.' ⁸ And the child grew, and was weaned; and Abraham made a great feast the same day that Isaac was weaned.

⁹ And Sarah saw the son of Hagar the Egyptian, which she had born unto Abraham, mocking. ¹⁰ Wherefore she said unto Abraham, 'Cast out this bondwoman and her son: for the son of this bondwoman shall not be heir with my son, even with Isaac.' ¹¹ And the thing was very grievous in Abraham's sight because of his son.

¹² And God said unto Abraham, 'Let it not be grievous in

thy sight because of the lad, and because of thy bondwoman; in all that Sarah hath said unto thee, hearken unto her voice; for in Isaac shall thy seed be called. ¹³And also of the son of the bondwoman will I make a nation, because he is thy seed.' ¹⁴And Abraham rose up early in the morning, and took bread, and a bottle of water, and gave it unto Hagar, putting it on her shoulder, and the child, and sent her away; and she departed, and wandered in the wilderness of Beer-sheba. ¹⁵And the water was spent in the bottle, and she cast the child under one of the shrubs. ¹⁶And she went, and sat her down over against him a good way off, as it were a bowshot; for she said, 'Let me not see the death of the child.' And she sat over against him, and lift up her voice, and wept. ¹⁷And God heard the voice of the lad; and the angel of God called to Hagar out of heaven, and said unto her, 'What aileth thee, Hagar? Fear not; for God hath heard the voice of the lad where he is. ¹⁸Arise, lift up the lad, and hold him in thine hand; for I will make him a great nation.' ¹⁹And God opened her eyes, and she saw a well of water; and she went, and filled the bottle with water, and gave the lad drink. ²⁰And God was with the lad; and he grew, and dwelt in the wilderness, and became an archer. ²¹And he dwelt in the wilderness of Paran; and his mother took him a wife out of the land of Egypt.

²²And it came to pass at that time, that Abimelech and Phichol the chief captain of his host spake unto Abraham, saying, 'God is with thee in all that thou doest; ²³ now therefore swear unto me here by God that thou wilt not deal falsely with me, nor with my son, nor with my son's son; but

according to the kindness that I have done unto thee, thou shalt do unto me, and to the land wherein thou hast sojourned.' ²⁴And Abraham said, 'I will swear.' ²⁵And Abraham reproved Abimelech because of a well of water, which Abimelech's servants had violently taken away. ²⁶And Abimelech said, 'I wot not who hath done this thing; neither didst thou tell me, neither yet heard I of it, but to day.' ²⁷And Abraham took sheep and oxen, and gave them unto Abimelech; and both of them made a covenant. ²⁸And Abraham set seven ewe lambs of the flock by themselves. ²⁹And Abimelech said unto Abraham, 'What mean these seven ewe lambs which thou hast set by themselves?' ³⁰And he said, 'For these seven ewe lambs shalt thou take of my hand, that they may be a witness unto me, that I have digged this well.' ³¹Wherefore he called that place Beer-sheba; because there they sware both of them. ³²Thus they made a covenant at Beer-sheba; then Abimelech rose up, and Phichol the chief captain of his host, and they returned into the land of the Philistines.

³³And Abraham planted a grove in Beer-sheba, and called there on the name of the Lord, the everlasting God. ³⁴And Abraham sojourned in the Philistines' land many days.

22 And it came to pass after these things, that God did tempt Abraham, and said unto him, 'Abraham,' and he said, 'Behold, here I am.' ²And he said, 'Take now thy son, thine only son Isaac, whom thou lovest, and get thee into the land of Moriah; and offer him there for a burnt offering upon one of the mountains which I will tell thee of.'

³And Abraham rose up early in the morning, and saddled his ass, and took two of his young men with him, and Isaac his son, and clave the wood for the burnt offering, and rose up, and went unto the place of which God had told him. ⁴Then on the third day Abraham lifted up his eyes, and saw the place afar off. ⁵And Abraham said unto his young men, 'Abide ye here with the ass; and I and the lad will go yonder and worship, and come again to you.' ⁶And Abraham took the wood of the burnt offering, and laid it upon Isaac his son; and he took the fire in his hand, and a knife; and they went both of them together. ⁷And Isaac spake unto Abraham his father, and said, 'My father,' and he said, 'Here am I, my son.' And Isaac said, 'Behold the fire and the wood; but where is the lamb for a burnt offering?' ⁸And Abraham said, 'My son, God will provide himself a lamb for a burnt offering'; so they went both of them together. ⁹And they came to the place which God had told him of; and Abraham built an altar there, and laid the wood in order, and bound Isaac his son, and laid him on the altar upon the wood. ¹⁰And Abraham stretched forth his hand, and took the knife to slay his son. ¹¹And the angel of the Lord called unto him out of heaven, and said, 'Abraham, Abraham,' and he said, 'Here am I.' ¹²And he said, 'Lay not thine hand upon the lad, neither do thou any thing unto him; for now I know that thou fearest God, seeing thou hast not withheld thy son, thine only son from me.' ¹³And Abraham lifted up his eyes, and looked, and behold behind him a ram caught in a thicket by his horns; and Abraham went and took the ram, and offered him up

for a burnt offering in the stead of his son. ¹⁴And Abraham called the name of that place Jehovah-jireh: as it is said to this day, in the mount of the Lord it shall be seen.

¹⁵And the angel of the Lord called unto Abraham out of heaven the second time, ¹⁶and said, 'By myself have I sworn, saith the Lord, for because thou hast done this thing, and hast not withheld thy son, thine only son: ¹⁷that in blessing I will bless thee, and in multiplying I will multiply thy seed as the stars of the heaven, and as the sand which is upon the sea shore; and thy seed shall possess the gate of his enemies; ¹⁸and in thy seed shall all the nations of the earth be blessed; because thou hast obeyed my voice.' ¹⁹So Abraham returned unto his young men, and they rose up and went together to Beer-sheba; and Abraham dwelt at Beer-sheba.

²⁰And it came to pass after these things, that it was told Abraham, saying, 'Behold, Milcah, she hath also born children unto thy brother Nahor; ²¹Huz his firstborn, and Buz his brother, and Kemuel the father of Aram, ²²and Chesed, and Hazo, and Pildash, and Jidlaph, and Bethuel. ²³And Bethuel begat Rebekah: these eight Milcah did bear to Nahor, Abraham's brother. ²⁴And his concubine, whose name was Reumah, she bare also Tebah, and Gaham, and Thahash, and Maachah.'

23 And Sarah was an hundred and seven and twenty years old: these were the years of the life of Sarah. ²And Sarah died in Kirjath-arba; the same is Hebron in the land of Canaan; and Abraham came to mourn for Sarah, and to weep for her.

³And Abraham stood up from before his dead, and spake unto the sons of Heth, saying, ⁴'I am a stranger and a sojourner with you; give me a possession of a buryingplace with you, that I may bury my dead out of my sight.' ⁵And the children of Heth answered Abraham, saying unto him, ⁶'Hear us, my lord: thou art a mighty prince among us; in the choice of our sepulchres bury thy dead; none of us shall withhold from thee his sepulchre, but that thou mayest bury thy dead.' ⁷And Abraham stood up, and bowed himself to the people of the land, even to the children of Heth. ⁸And he communed with them, saying, 'If it be your mind that I should bury my dead out of my sight; hear me, and intreat for me to Ephron the son of Zohar, ⁹that he may give me the cave of Machpelah, which he hath, which is in the end of his field; for as much money as it is worth he shall give it me for a possession of a buryingplace amongst you.' ¹⁰And Ephron dwelt among the children of Heth: and Ephron the Hittite answered Abraham in the audience of the children of Heth, even of all that went in at the gate of his city, saying, ¹¹'Nay, my lord, hear me: the field give I thee, and the cave that is therein, I give it thee; in the presence of the sons of my people give I it thee; bury thy dead.' ¹²And Abraham bowed down himself before the people of the land. ¹³And he spake unto Ephron in the audience of the people of the land, saying, 'But if thou wilt give it, I pray thee, hear me: I will give thee money for the field; take it of me, and I will bury my dead there.' ¹⁴And Ephron answered Abraham, saying unto him, ¹⁵'My lord, hearken unto me: the land is worth four hundred

shekels of silver; what is that betwixt me and thee? Bury therefore thy dead.' ¹⁶And Abraham hearkened unto Ephron; and Abraham weighed to Ephron the silver, which he had named in the audience of the sons of Heth, four hundred shekels of silver, current money with the merchant.

¹⁷And the field of Ephron, which was in Machpelah, which was before Mamre, the field, and the cave which was therein, and all the trees that were in the field, that were in all the borders round about, were made sure ¹⁸ unto Abraham for a possession in the presence of the children of Heth, before all that went in at the gate of his city. ¹⁹And after this, Abraham buried Sarah his wife in the cave of the field of Machpelah before Mamre: the same is Hebron in the land of Canaan. ²⁰And the field, and the cave that is therein, were made sure unto Abraham for a possession of a buryingplace by the sons of Heth.

24 And Abraham was old, and well stricken in age: and the Lord had blessed Abraham in all things. ²And Abraham said unto his eldest servant of his house, that ruled over all that he had, 'Put, I pray thee, thy hand under my thigh; ³and I will make thee swear by the Lord, the God of heaven, and the God of the earth, that thou shalt not take a wife unto my son of the daughters of the Canaanites, among whom I dwell; ⁴but thou shalt go unto my country, and to my kindred, and take a wife unto my son Isaac.' ⁵And the servant said unto him, 'Peradventure the woman will not be willing to follow me unto this land; must I needs bring thy

son again unto the land from whence thou camest?' ⁶And Abraham said unto him, 'Beware thou that thou bring not my son thither again.

⁷'The Lord God of heaven, which took me from my father's house, and from the land of my kindred, and which spake unto me, and that sware unto me, saying, "Unto thy seed will I give this land"; he shall send his angel before thee, and thou shalt take a wife unto my son from thence. ⁸And if the woman will not be willing to follow thee, then thou shalt be clear from this my oath: only bring not my son thither again.' ⁹And the servant put his hand under the thigh of Abraham his master, and sware to him concerning that matter.

¹⁰And the servant took ten camels of the camels of his master, and departed; for all the goods of his master were in his hand; and he arose, and went to Mesopotamia, unto the city of Nahor. ¹¹And he made his camels to kneel down without the city by a well of water at the time of the evening, even the time that women go out to draw water. ¹²And he said, 'O Lord God of my master Abraham, I pray thee, send me good speed this day, and shew kindness unto my master Abraham. ¹³Behold, I stand here by the well of water; and the daughters of the men of the city come out to draw water; ¹⁴and let it come to pass that the damsel to whom I shall say, "Let down thy pitcher, I pray thee, that I may drink"; and she shall say, "Drink, and I will give thy camels drink also"; let the same be she that thou hast appointed for thy servant Isaac; and thereby shall I know that thou hast shewed kindness unto my master.'

¹⁵And it came to pass, before he had done speaking, that, behold, Rebekah came out, who was born to Bethuel, son of Milcah, the wife of Nahor, Abraham's brother, with her pitcher upon her shoulder. ¹⁶And the damsel was very fair to look upon, a virgin, neither had any man known her; and she went down to the well, and filled her pitcher, and came up. ¹⁷And the servant ran to meet her, and said, 'Let me, I pray thee, drink a little water of thy pitcher.' ¹⁸And she said, 'Drink, my lord'; and she hasted, and let down her pitcher upon her hand, and gave him drink. ¹⁹And when she had done giving him drink, she said, 'I will draw water for thy camels also, until they have done drinking.' ²⁰And she hasted, and emptied her pitcher into the trough, and ran again unto the well to draw water, and drew for all his camels. ²¹And the man wondering at her held his peace, to wit whether the Lord had made his journey prosperous or not. ²²And it came to pass, as the camels had done drinking, that the man took a golden earring of half a shekel weight, and two bracelets for her hands of ten shekels weight of gold; ²³and said, 'Whose daughter art thou? Tell me, I pray thee; is there room in thy father's house for us to lodge in?' ²⁴And she said unto him, 'I am the daughter of Bethuel the son of Milcah, which she bare unto Nahor.' ²⁵She said moreover unto him, 'We have both straw and provender enough, and room to lodge in.' ²⁶And the man bowed down his head, and worshipped the Lord. ²⁷And he said, 'Blessed be the Lord God of my master Abraham, who hath not left destitute my master of his mercy and his truth; I being in the way, the Lord led me to the house of

my master's brethren.' ²⁸And the damsel ran, and told them of her mother's house these things.

²⁹And Rebekah had a brother, and his name was Laban; and Laban ran out unto the man, unto the well. ³⁰And it came to pass, when he saw the earring and bracelets upon his sister's hands, and when he heard the words of Rebekah his sister, saying, 'Thus spake the man unto me'; that he came unto the man; and, behold, he stood by the camels at the well. ³¹And he said, 'Come in, thou blessed of the Lord; wherefore standest thou without? For I have prepared the house, and room for the camels.'

³²And the man came into the house; and he ungirded his camels, and gave straw and provender for the camels, and water to wash his feet, and the men's feet that were with him. ³³And there was set meat before him to eat; but he said, 'I will not eat, until I have told mine errand.' And he said, 'Speak on.' ³⁴And he said, 'I am Abraham's servant. ³⁵And the Lord hath blessed my master greatly; and he is become great; and he hath given him flocks, and herds, and silver, and gold, and menservants, and maidservants, and camels, and asses. ³⁶And Sarah my master's wife bare a son to my master when she was old; and unto him hath he given all that he hath. ³⁷And my master made me swear, saying, "Thou shalt not take a wife to my son of the daughters of the Canaanites, in whose land I dwell; ³⁸but thou shalt go unto my father's house, and to my kindred, and take a wife unto my son." ³⁹And I said unto my master, "Peradventure the woman will not follow me." ⁴⁰And he said unto me, "The Lord, before whom I

walk, will send his angel with thee, and prosper thy way; and thou shalt take a wife for my son of my kindred, and of my father's house; [41] then shalt thou be clear from this my oath, when thou comest to my kindred; and if they give not thee one, thou shalt be clear from my oath." [42] And I came this day unto the well, and said, "O Lord God of my master z I stand by the well of water; and it shall come to pass, that when the virgin cometh forth to draw water, and I say to her, 'Give me, I pray thee, a little water of thy pitcher to drink'; [44] And she say to me, 'Both drink thou, and I will also draw for thy camels': let the same be the woman whom the Lord hath appointed out for my master's son." [45] And before I had done speaking in mine heart, behold, Rebekah came forth with her pitcher on her shoulder; and she went down unto the well, and drew water; and I said unto her, "Let me drink, I pray thee." [46] And she made haste, and let down her pitcher from her shoulder, and said, "Drink, and I will give thy camels drink also"; so I drank, and she made the camels drink also. [47] And I asked her, and said, "Whose daughter art thou?" And she said, "The daughter of Bethuel, Nahor's son, whom Milcah bare unto him"; and I put the earring upon her face, and the bracelets upon her hands. [48] And I bowed down my head, and worshipped the Lord, and blessed the Lord God of my master Abraham, which had led me in the right way to take my master's brother's daughter unto his son. [49] And now if ye will deal kindly and truly with my master, tell me; and if not, tell me; that I may turn to the right hand, or to the left.'

⁵⁰ Then Laban and Bethuel answered and said, 'The thing proceedeth from the Lord; we cannot speak unto thee bad or good. ⁵¹ Behold, Rebekah is before thee, take her, and go, and let her be thy master's son's wife, as the Lord hath spoken.' ⁵²And it came to pass, that, when Abraham's servant heard their words, he worshipped the Lord, bowing himself to the earth. ⁵³And the servant brought forth jewels of silver, and jewels of gold, and raiment, and gave them to Rebekah; he gave also to her brother and to her mother precious things. ⁵⁴And they did eat and drink, he and the men that were with him, and tarried all night; and they rose up in the morning, and he said, 'Send me away unto my master.' ⁵⁵And her brother and her mother said, 'Let the damsel abide with us a few days, at the least ten; after that she shall go.' ⁵⁶And he said unto them, 'Hinder me not, seeing the Lord hath prospered my way; send me away that I may go to my master.' ⁵⁷And they said, 'We will call the damsel, and enquire at her mouth.' ⁵⁸And they called Rebekah, and said unto her, 'Wilt thou go with this man?' And she said, 'I will go.' ⁵⁹And they sent away Rebekah their sister, and her nurse, and Abraham's servant, and his men. ⁶⁰And they blessed Rebekah, and said unto her, 'Thou art our sister, be thou the mother of thousands of millions, and let thy seed possess the gate of those which hate them.'

⁶¹And Rebekah arose, and her damsels, and they rode upon the camels, and followed the man; and the servant took Rebekah, and went his way. ⁶²And Isaac came from the way of the well Lahai-roi; for he dwelt in the south country.

⁶³And Isaac went out to meditate in the field at the eventide: and he lifted up his eyes, and saw, and, behold, the camels were coming. ⁶⁴And Rebekah lifted up her eyes, and when she saw Isaac, she lighted off the camel. ⁶⁵For she had said unto the servant, 'What man is this that walketh in the field to meet us?' And the servant had said, 'It is my master'; therefore she took a vail, and covered herself. ⁶⁶And the servant told Isaac all things that he had done. ⁶⁷And Isaac brought her into his mother Sarah's tent, and took Rebekah, and she became his wife; and he loved her; and Isaac was comforted after his mother's death.

25 Then again Abraham took a wife, and her name was Keturah. ²And she bare him Zimran, and Jokshan, and Medan, and Midian, and Ishbak, and Shuah. ³And Jokshan begat Sheba, and Dedan. And the sons of Dedan were Asshurim, and Letushim, and Leummim. ⁴And the sons of Midian: Ephah, and Epher, and Hanoch, and Abida, and Eldaah. All these were the children of Keturah.

⁵And Abraham gave all that he had unto Isaac. ⁶But unto the sons of the concubines, which Abraham had, Abraham gave gifts, and sent them away from Isaac his son, while he yet lived, eastward, unto the east country. ⁷And these are the days of the years of Abraham's life which he lived, an hundred threescore and fifteen years. ⁸Then Abraham gave up the ghost, and died in a good old age, an old man, and full of years; and was gathered to his people. ⁹And his sons Isaac and Ishmael buried him in the cave of Machpelah, in the

field of Ephron the son of Zohar the Hittite, which is before Mamre; [10] the field which Abraham purchased of the sons of Heth; there was Abraham buried, and Sarah his wife.

[11] And it came to pass after the death of Abraham, that God blessed his son Isaac; and Isaac dwelt by the well Lahai-roi.

[12] Now these are the generations of Ishmael, Abraham's son, whom Hagar the Egyptian, Sarah's handmaid, bare unto Abraham; [13] and these are the names of the sons of Ishmael, by their names, according to their generations: the firstborn of Ishmael, Nebajoth; and Kedar, and Adbeel, and Mibsam, [14] and Mishma, and Dumah, and Massa, [15] Hadar, and Tema, Jetur, Naphish, and Kedemah. [16] These are the sons of Ishmael, and these are their names, by their towns, and by their castles; twelve princes according to their nations. [17] And these are the years of the life of Ishmael, an hundred and thirty and seven years; and he gave up the ghost and died; and was gathered unto his people. [18] And they dwelt from Havilah unto Shur, that is before Egypt, as thou goest toward Assyria; and he died in the presence of all his brethren.

[19] And these are the generations of Isaac, Abraham's son: Abraham begat Isaac; [20] and Isaac was forty years old when he took Rebekah to wife, the daughter of Bethuel the Syrian of Padan-aram, the sister to Laban the Syrian. [21] And Isaac intreated the Lord for his wife, because she was barren; and the Lord was intreated of him, and Rebekah his wife conceived. [22] And the children struggled together within her; and she said, 'If it be so, why am I thus?' And she went to enquire of the Lord. [23] And the Lord said unto her, 'Two nations are

in thy womb, and two manner of people shall be separated from thy bowels; and the one people shall be stronger than the other people; and the elder shall serve the younger.'

²⁴And when her days to be delivered were fulfilled, behold, there were twins in her womb. ²⁵And the first came out red, all over like an hairy garment; and they called his name Esau. ²⁶And after that came his brother out, and his hand took hold on Esau's heel; and his name was called Jacob; and Isaac was threescore years old when she bare them. ²⁷And the boys grew; and Esau was a cunning hunter, a man of the field; and Jacob was a plain man, dwelling in tents. ²⁸And Isaac loved Esau, because he did eat of his venison; but Rebekah loved Jacob.

²⁹And Jacob sod pottage; and Esau came from the field, and he was faint; ³⁰and Esau said to Jacob, 'Feed me, I pray thee, with that same red pottage; for I am faint'; therefore was his name called Edom. ³¹And Jacob said, 'Sell me this day thy birthright.' ³²And Esau said, 'Behold, I am at the point to die; and what profit shall this birthright do to me?' ³³And Jacob said, 'Swear to me this day'; and Esau sware unto him; and he sold his birthright unto Jacob. ³⁴Then Jacob gave Esau bread and pottage of lentiles; and he did eat and drink, and rose up, and went his way; thus Esau despised his birthright.

26 And there was a famine in the land, beside the first famine that was in the days of Abraham. And Isaac went unto Abimelech king of the Philistines unto Gerar. ²And the Lord appeared unto him, and said, 'Go not down into

Egypt; dwell in the land which I shall tell thee of; ³ sojourn in this land, and I will be with thee, and will bless thee; for unto thee, and unto thy seed, I will give all these countries, and I will perform the oath which I sware unto Abraham thy father; ⁴ and I will make thy seed to multiply as the stars of heaven, and will give unto thy seed all these countries; and in thy seed shall all the nations of the earth be blessed; ⁵ because that Abraham obeyed my voice, and kept my charge, my commandments, my statues, and my laws.'

⁶ And Isaac dwelt in Gerar. ⁷ And the men of the place asked him of his wife; and he said, 'She is my sister', for he feared to say, 'She is my wife', lest, said he, 'the men of the place should kill me for Rebekah;' because she was fair to look upon. ⁸ And it came to pass, when he had been there a long time, that Abimelech king of the Philistines looked out at a window, and saw, and, behold, Isaac was sporting with Rebekah his wife. ⁹ And Abimelech called Isaac, and said, 'Behold, of a surety she is thy wife: and how saidst thou, "She is my sister"?' And Isaac said unto him, 'Because I said, Lest I die for her.' ¹⁰ And Abimelech said, 'What is this thou hast done unto us? One of the people might lightly have lien with thy wife, and thou shouldest have brought guiltiness upon us.' ¹¹ And Abimelech charged all his people, saying, 'He that toucheth this man or his wife shall surely be put to death.' ¹² Then Isaac sowed in that land, and received in the same year an hundred-fold: and the Lord blessed him. ¹³ And the man waxed great, and went forward, and grew until he became very great; ¹⁴ for he had possession of flocks, and

possession of herds, and great store of servants: and the Philistines envied him. ¹⁵ For all the wells which his father's servants had digged in the days of Abraham his father, the Philistines had stopped them, and filled them with earth. ¹⁶And Abimelech said unto Isaac, 'Go from us; for thou art much mightier than we.'

¹⁷And Isaac departed thence, and pitched his tent in the valley of Gerar, and dwelt there. ¹⁸And Isaac digged again the wells of water, which they had digged in the days of Abraham his father; for the Philistines had stopped them after the death of Abraham; and he called their names after the names by which his father had called them. ¹⁹And Isaac's servants digged in the valley, and found there a well of springing water. ²⁰And the herdmen of Gerar did strive with Isaac's herdmen, saying, 'The water is ours,' and he called the name of the well Esek; because they strove with him. ²¹And they digged another well, and strove for that also; and he called the name of it Sitnah. ²²And he removed from thence, and digged another well; and for that they strove not; and he called the name of it Rehoboth; and he said, 'For now the Lord hath made room for us, and we shall be fruitful in the land.' ²³And he went up from thence to Beer-sheba. ²⁴And the Lord appeared unto him the same night, and said, 'I am the God of Abraham thy father: fear not, for I am with thee, and will bless thee, and multiply thy seed for my servant Abraham's sake.' ²⁵And he builded an altar there, and called upon the name of the Lord, and pitched his tent there; and there Isaac's servants digged a well.

²⁶ Then Abimelech went to him from Gerar, and Ahuzzath one of his friends, and Phichol the chief captain of his army. ²⁷And Isaac said unto them, 'Wherefore come ye to me, seeing ye hate me, and have sent me away from you?' ²⁸And they said, 'We saw certainly that the Lord was with thee; and we said, "Let there be now an oath betwixt us, even betwixt us and thee, and let us make a covenant with thee"; ²⁹ that thou wilt do us no hurt, as we have not touched thee, and as we have done unto thee nothing but good, and have sent thee away in peace: thou art now the blessed of the Lord.' ³⁰And he made them a feast, and they did eat and drink. ³¹And they rose up betimes in the morning, and sware one to another; and Isaac sent them away, and they departed from him in peace. ³²And it came to pass the same day, that Isaac's servants came, and told him concerning the well which they had digged, and said unto him, 'We have found water.' ³³And he called it Shebah: therefore the name of the city is Beer-sheba unto this day.

³⁴And Esau was forty years old when he took to wife Judith the daughter of Beeri the Hittite, and Bashemath the daughter of Elon the Hittite: ³⁵ which were a grief of mind unto Isaac and to Rebekah.

27 And it came to pass that, when Isaac was old, and his eyes were dim, so that he could not see, he called Esau his eldest son, and said unto him, 'My son,' and he said unto him, 'Behold, here am I.' ²And Isaac said, 'Behold now, I am old, I know not the day of my death; ³ now therefore

take, I pray thee, thy weapons, thy quiver and thy bow, and go out to the field, and take me some venison; ^{4} and make me savoury meat, such as I love, and bring it to me, that I may eat; that my soul may bless thee before I die.' ^{5} And Rebekah heard when Isaac spake to Esau his son. And Esau went to the field to hunt for venison, and to bring it.

^{6} And Rebekah spake unto Jacob her son, saying, 'Behold, I heard thy father speak unto Esau thy brother, saying, ^{7} "Bring me venison, and make me savoury meat, that I may eat, and bless thee before the Lord before my death." ^{8} Now therefore, my son, obey my voice according to that which I command thee. ^{9} Go now to the flock, and fetch me from thence two good kids of the goats; and I will make them savoury meat for thy father, such as he loveth; ^{10} and thou shalt bring it to thy father, that he may eat, and that he may bless thee before his death.' ^{11} And Jacob said to Rebekah his mother, 'Behold, Esau my brother is a hairy man, and I am a smooth man: ^{12} my father peradventure will feel me, and I shall seem to him as a deceiver; and I shall bring a curse upon me, and not a blessing.' ^{13} And his mother said unto him, 'Upon me be thy curse, my son; only obey my voice, and go fetch me them.' ^{14} And he went, and fetched, and brought them to his mother; and his mother made savoury meat, such as his father loved. ^{15} And Rebekah took goodly raiment of her eldest son Esau, which were with her in the house, and put them upon Jacob her younger son; ^{16} and she put the skins of the kids of the goats upon his hands, and upon the smooth of his neck; ^{17} and she gave the savoury meat and the bread, which she had prepared, into the hand of her son Jacob.

¹⁸And he came unto his father, and said, 'My father,' and he said, 'Here am I; who art thou, my son?' ¹⁹And Jacob said unto his father, 'I am Esau thy firstborn; I have done according as thou badest me; arise, I pray thee, sit and eat of my venison, that thy soul may bless me.' ²⁰And Isaac said unto his son, 'How is it that thou hast found it so quickly, my son?' And he said, 'Because the Lord thy God brought it to me.' ²¹And Isaac said unto Jacob, 'Come near, I pray thee, that I may feel thee, my son, whether thou be my very son Esau or not.' ²²And Jacob went near unto Isaac his father; and he felt him, and said, 'The voice is Jacob's voice, but the hands are the hands of Esau.' ²³And he discerned him not, because his hands were hairy, as his brother Esau's hands; so he blessed him. ²⁴And he said, 'Art thou my very son Esau?' And he said, 'I am.' ²⁵And Isaac said, 'Bring it near to me, and I will eat of my son's venison, that my soul may bless thee.' And he brought it near to him, and he did eat; and he brought him wine, and he drank. ²⁶And his father Isaac said unto him, 'Come near now, and kiss me, my son.' ²⁷And he came near, and kissed him: and he smelled the smell of his raiment, and blessed him, and said, 'See, the smell of my son is as the smell of a field which the Lord hath blessed; ²⁸therefore God give thee of the dew of heaven, and the fatness of the earth, and plenty of corn and wine; ²⁹let people serve thee, and nations bow down to thee; be lord over thy brethren, and let thy mother's sons bow down to thee; cursed be every one that curseth thee, and blessed be he that blesseth thee.'

³⁰And it came to pass, as soon as Isaac had made an end of blessing Jacob, and Jacob was yet scarce gone out from the presence of Isaac his father, that Esau his brother came in from his hunting. ³¹And he also had made savoury meat, and brought it unto his father, and said unto his father, 'Let my father arise, and eat of his son's venison, that thy soul may bless me.' ³²And Isaac his father said unto him, 'Who art thou?' And he said, 'I am thy son, thy firstborn Esau.' ³³And Isaac trembled very exceedingly, and said, 'Who? Where is he that hath taken venison, and brought it me, and I have eaten of all before thou camest, and have blessed him? Yea, and he shall be blessed.' ³⁴And when Esau heard the words of his father, he cried with a great and exceeding bitter cry, and said unto his father, 'Bless me, even me also, O my father.' ³⁵And he said, 'Thy brother came with subtilty, and hath taken away thy blessing.' ³⁶And Esau said, 'Is not he rightly named Jacob? For he hath supplanted me these two times: he took away my birthright; and, behold, now he hath taken away my blessing.' And he said, 'Hast thou not reserved a blessing for me?' ³⁷And Isaac answered and said unto Esau, 'Behold, I have made him thy lord, and all his brethren have I given to him for servants; and with corn and wine have I sustained him: and what shall I do now unto thee, my son?' ³⁸And Esau said unto his father, 'Hast thou but one blessing, my father? Bless me, even me also, O my father.' And Esau lifted up his voice, and wept. ³⁹And Isaac his father answered and said unto him, 'Behold, thy dwelling shall be the fatness of the earth, and of the dew of heaven from above; ⁴⁰and by

thy sword shalt thou live, and shalt serve thy brother; and it shall come to pass when thou shalt have the dominion, that thou shalt break his yoke from off thy neck.'

⁴¹And Esau hated Jacob because of the blessing wherewith his father blessed him; and Esau said in his heart, 'The days of mourning for my father are at hand; then will I slay my brother Jacob.' ⁴²And these words of Esau her elder son were told to Rebekah; and she sent and called Jacob her younger son, and said unto him, 'Behold, thy brother Esau, as touching thee, doth comfort himself, purposing to kill thee. ⁴³ Now therefore, my son, obey my voice; and arise, flee thou to Laban my brother to Haran; ⁴⁴and tarry with him a few days, until thy brother's fury turn away; ⁴⁵ until thy brother's anger turn away from thee, and he forget that which thou hast done to him; then I will send, and fetch thee from thence; why should I be deprived also of you both in one day?' ⁴⁶And Rebekah said to Isaac, 'I am weary of my life because of the daughters of Heth; if Jacob take a wife of the daughters of Heth, such as these which are of the daughters of the land, what good shall my life do me?'

28 And Isaac called Jacob, and blessed him, and charged him, and said unto him, 'Thou shalt not take a wife of the daughters of Canaan. ²Arise, go to Padan-aram, to the house of Bethuel thy mother's father; and take thee a wife from thence of the daughters of Laban thy mother's brother. ³And God Almighty bless thee, and make thee fruitful, and multiply thee, that thou mayest be a multitude of people;

⁴and give thee the blessing of Abraham, to thee, and to thy seed with thee; that thou mayest inherit the land wherein thou art a stranger, which God gave unto Abraham.' ⁵And Isaac sent away Jacob; and he went to Padan-aram unto Laban, son of Bethuel the Syrian, the brother of Rebekah, Jacob's and Esau's mother.

⁶ When Esau saw that Isaac had blessed Jacob, and sent him away to Padan-aram, to take him a wife from thence; and that as he blessed him he gave him a charge, saying, 'Thou shalt not take a wife of the daughters of Canaan,' ⁷and that Jacob obeyed his father and his mother, and was gone to Padan-aram; ⁸and Esau seeing that the daughters of Canaan pleased not Isaac his father; ⁹then went Esau unto Ishmael, and took unto the wives which he had Mahalath the daughter of Ishmael Abraham's son, the sister of Nebajoth, to be his wife.

¹⁰And Jacob went out from Beer-sheba, and went toward Haran. ¹¹And he lighted upon a certain place, and tarried there all night, because the sun was set; and he took of the stones of that place, and put them for his pillows, and lay down in that place to sleep. ¹²And he dreamed, and behold a ladder set up on the earth, and the top of it reached to heaven: and behold the angels of God ascending and descending on it. ¹³And, behold, the Lord stood above it, and said, 'I am the Lord God of Abraham thy father, and the God of Isaac: the land whereon thou liest, to thee will I give it, and to thy seed; ¹⁴and thy seed shall be as the dust of the earth, and thou shalt spread abroad to the west, and to the east, and to the

north, and to the south; and in thee and in thy seed shall all the families of the earth be blessed. ¹⁵And, behold, I am with thee, and will keep thee in all places whither thou goest, and will bring thee again into this land; for I will not leave thee, until I have done that which I have spoken to thee of.'

¹⁶And Jacob awaked out of his sleep, and he said, 'Surely the Lord is in this place; and I knew it not.' ¹⁷And he was afraid, and said, 'How dreadful is this place! This is none other but the house of God, and this is the gate of heaven.' ¹⁸And Jacob rose up early in the morning, and took the stone that he had put for his pillows, and set it up for a pillar, and poured oil upon the top of it. ¹⁹And he called the name of that place Beth-el: but the name of that city was called Luz at the first. ²⁰And Jacob vowed a vow, saying, 'If God will be with me, and will keep me in this way that I go, and will give me bread to eat, and raiment to put on, ²¹so that I come again to my father's house in peace; then shall the Lord be my God; ²²and this stone, which I have set for a pillar, shall be God's house; and of all that thou shalt give me I will surely give the tenth unto thee.'

29 Then Jacob went on his journey, and came into the land of the people of the east. ²And he looked, and behold a well in the field, and, lo, there were three flocks of sheep lying by it; for out of that well they watered the flocks; and a great stone was upon the well's mouth. ³And thither were all the flocks gathered; and they rolled the stone from the well's mouth, and watered the sheep, and put the stone

again upon the well's mouth in his place. ⁴And Jacob said unto them, 'My brethren, whence be ye?' And they said, 'Of Haran are we.' ⁵And he said unto them, 'Know ye Laban the son of Nahor?' And they said, 'We know him.' ⁶And he said unto them, 'Is he well?' And they said, 'He is well; and, behold, Rachel his daughter cometh with the sheep.' ⁷And he said, 'Lo, it is yet high day, neither is it time that the cattle should be gathered together; water ye the sheep, and go and feed them.' ⁸And they said, 'We cannot, until all the flocks be gathered together, and till they roll the stone from the well's mouth; then we water the sheep.'

⁹And while he yet spake with them, Rachel came with her father's sheep; for she kept them. ¹⁰And it came to pass, when Jacob saw Rachel the daughter of Laban his mother's brother, and the sheep of Laban his mother's brother, that Jacob went near, and rolled the stone from the well's mouth, and watered the flock of Laban his mother's brother. ¹¹And Jacob kissed Rachel, and lifted up his voice, and wept. ¹²And Jacob told Rachel that he was her father's brother, and that he was Rebekah's son; and she ran and told her father. ¹³And it came to pass, when Laban heard the tidings of Jacob his sister's son, that he ran to meet him, and embraced him, and kissed him, and brought him to his house. And he told Laban all these things. ¹⁴And Laban said to him, 'Surely thou art my bone and my flesh.' And he abode with him the space of a month.

¹⁵And Laban said unto Jacob, 'Because thou art my brother, shouldest thou therefore serve me for nought? Tell me, what shall thy wages be?' ¹⁶And Laban had two daughters: the

name of the elder was Leah, and the name of the younger was Rachel. ¹⁷Leah was tender eyed; but Rachel was beautiful and well favoured. ¹⁸And Jacob loved Rachel; and said, 'I will serve thee seven years for Rachel thy younger daughter.' ¹⁹And Laban said, 'It is better that I give her to thee, than that I should give her to another man: abide with me.' ²⁰And Jacob served seven years for Rachel; and they seemed unto him but a few days, for the love he had to her.

²¹And Jacob said unto Laban, 'Give me my wife, for my days are fulfilled, that I may go in unto her.' ²²And Laban gathered together all the men of the place, and made a feast. ²³And it came to pass in the evening, that he took Leah his daughter, and brought her to him; and he went in unto her. ²⁴And Laban gave unto his daughter Leah Zilpah his maid for an handmaid. ²⁵And it came to pass that in the morning, behold, it was Leah: and he said to Laban, 'What is this thou hast done unto me? Did not I serve with thee for Rachel? Wherefore then hast thou beguiled me?' ²⁶And Laban said, 'It must not be so done in our country, to give the younger before the firstborn. ²⁷Fulfil her week, and we will give thee this also for the service which thou shalt serve with me yet seven other years.' ²⁸And Jacob did so, and fulfilled her week; and he gave him Rachel his daughter to wife also. ²⁹And Laban gave to Rachel his daughter Bilhah his handmaid to be her maid. ³⁰And he went in also unto Rachel, and he loved also Rachel more than Leah, and served with him yet seven other years.

³¹And when the Lord saw that Leah was hated, he opened

her womb: but Rachel was barren. ³²And Leah conceived, and bare a son, and she called his name Reuben; for she said, 'Surely the Lord hath looked upon my affliction; now therefore my husband will love me.' ³³And she conceived again, and bare a son; and said, 'Because the Lord hath heard that I was hated, he hath therefore given me this son also', and she called his name Simeon. ³⁴And she conceived again, and bare a son; and said, 'Now this time will my husband be joined unto me, because I have born him three sons'; therefore was his name called Levi. ³⁵And she conceived again, and bare a son; and she said, 'Now will I praise the Lord'; therefore she called his name Judah; and left bearing.

30 And when Rachel saw that she bare Jacob no children, Rachel envied her sister; and said unto Jacob, 'Give me children, or else I die.' ²And Jacob's anger was kindled against Rachel; and he said, 'Am I in God's stead, who hath withheld from thee the fruit of the womb?' ³And she said, 'Behold my maid Bilhah, go in unto her; and she shall bear upon my knees, that I may also have children by her.' ⁴And she gave him Bilhah her handmaid to wife; and Jacob went in unto her. ⁵And Bilhah conceived, and bare Jacob a son. ⁶And Rachel said, 'God hath judged me, and hath also heard my voice, and hath given me a son'; therefore called she his name Dan. ⁷And Bilhah Rachel's maid conceived again, and bare Jacob a second son. ⁸And Rachel said, 'With great wrestlings have I wrestled with my sister, and I have prevailed'; and she called his name Naphtali. ⁹When Leah

saw that she had left bearing, she took Zilpah her maid, and gave her Jacob to wife. ¹⁰And Zilpah Leah's maid bare Jacob a son. ¹¹And Leah said, 'A troop cometh', and she called his name Gad. ¹²And Zilpah Leah's maid bare Jacob a second son. ¹³And Leah said, 'Happy am I, for the daughters will call me blessed,' and she called his name Asher.

¹⁴And Reuben went in the days of wheat harvest, and found mandrakes in the field, and brought them unto his mother Leah. Then Rachel said to Leah, 'Give me, I pray thee, of thy son's mandrakes.' ¹⁵And she said unto her, 'Is it a small matter that thou hast taken my husband? And wouldest thou take away my son's mandrakes also?' And Rachel said, 'Therefore he shall lie with thee to night for thy son's mandrakes.' ¹⁶And Jacob came out of the field in the evening, and Leah went out to meet him, and said, 'Thou must come in unto me; for surely I have hired thee with my son's mandrakes.' And he lay with her that night. ¹⁷And God hearkened unto Leah, and she conceived, and bare Jacob the fifth son. ¹⁸And Leah said, 'God hath given me my hire, because I have given my maiden to my husband,' and she called his name Issachar. ¹⁹And Leah conceived again, and bare Jacob the sixth son. ²⁰And Leah said, 'God hath endued me with a good dowry; now will my husband dwell with me, because I have born him six sons,' and she called his name Zebulun. ²¹And afterwards she bare a daughter, and called her name Dinah.

²²And God remembered Rachel, and God hearkened to her, and opened her womb. ²³And she conceived, and bare a son; and said, 'God hath taken away my reproach,' ²⁴and she

called his name Joseph; and said, 'The Lord shall add to me another son.'

²⁵And it came to pass, when Rachel had born Joseph, that Jacob said unto Laban, 'Send me away, that I may go unto mine own place, and to my country. ²⁶Give me my wives and my children, for whom I have served thee, and let me go; for thou knowest my service which I have done thee.' ²⁷And Laban said unto him, 'I pray thee, if I have found favour in thine eyes, tarry: for I have learned by experience that the Lord hath blessed me for thy sake.' ²⁸And he said, 'Appoint me thy wages, and I will give it.' ²⁹And Jacob said unto him, 'Thou knowest how I have served thee, and how thy cattle was with me. ³⁰For it was little which thou hadst before I came, and it is now increased unto a multitude; and the Lord hath blessed thee since my coming; and now when shall I provide for mine own house also?' ³¹And Laban said, 'What shall I give thee?' And Jacob said, 'Thou shalt not give me any thing; if thou wilt do this thing for me, I will again feed and keep thy flock. ³²I will pass through all thy flock to day, removing from thence all the speckled and spotted cattle, and all the brown cattle among the sheep, and the spotted and speckled among the goats; and of such shall be my hire. ³³So shall my righteousness answer for me in time to come, when it shall come for my hire before thy face; every one that is not speckled and spotted among the goats, and brown among the sheep, that shall be counted stolen with me.' ³⁴And Laban said, 'Behold, I would it might be according to thy word.' ³⁵And he removed that day the he goats

that were ringstraked and spotted, and all the she goats that were speckled and spotted, and every one that had some white in it, and all the brown among the sheep, and gave them into the hand of his sons. ³⁶And he set three days' journey betwixt himself and Jacob: and Jacob fed the rest of Laban's flocks.

³⁷And Jacob took him rods of green poplar, and of the hazel and chesnut tree; and pilled white strakes in them, and made the white appear which was in the rods. ³⁸And he set the rods which he had pilled before the flocks in the gutters in the watering troughs when the flocks came to drink, that they should conceive when they came to drink. ³⁹And the flocks conceived before the rods, and brought forth cattle ringstraked, speckled, and spotted. ⁴⁰And Jacob did separate the lambs, and set the faces of the flocks toward the ringstraked, and all the brown in the flock of Laban; and he put his own flocks by themselves, and put them not unto Laban's cattle. ⁴¹And it came to pass, whensoever the stronger cattle did conceive, that Jacob laid the rods before the eyes of the cattle in the gutters, that they might conceive among the rods. ⁴²But when the cattle were feeble, he put them not in: so the feebler were Laban's, and the stronger Jacob's. ⁴³And the man increased exceedingly, and had much cattle, and maidservants, and menservants, and camels, and asses.

31 And Jacob heard the words of Laban's sons, saying, 'Jacob hath taken away all that was our father's; and of that which was our father's hath he gotten all this glory.'

²And Jacob beheld the countenance of Laban, and, behold, it was not toward him as before. ³And the Lord said unto Jacob, 'Return unto the land of thy fathers, and to thy kindred; and I will be with thee.' ⁴And Jacob sent and called Rachel and Leah to the field unto his flock, ⁵and said unto them, 'I see your father's countenance, that it is not toward me as before; but the God of my father hath been with me. ⁶And ye know that with all my power I have served your father. ⁷And your father hath deceived me, and changed my wages ten times; but God suffered him not to hurt me. ⁸If he said thus, "The speckled shall be thy wages," then all the cattle bare speckled: and if he said thus, "The ringstraked shall be thy hire," then bare all the cattle ringstraked. ⁹Thus God hath taken away the cattle of your father, and given them to me. ¹⁰And it came to pass at the time that the cattle conceived, that I lifted up mine eyes, and saw in a dream, and, behold, the rams which leaped upon the cattle were ringstraked, speckled, and grisled. ¹¹And the angel of God spake unto me in a dream, saying, "Jacob," and I said, "Here am I." ¹²And he said, "Lift up now thine eyes, and see, all the rams which leap upon the cattle are ringstraked, speckled, and grisled; for I have seen all that Laban doeth unto thee. ¹³I am the God of Beth-el, where thou anointedst the pillar, and where thou vowedst a vow unto me; now arise, get thee out from this land, and return unto the land of thy kindred."' ¹⁴And Rachel and Leah answered and said unto him, 'Is there yet any portion or inheritance for us in our father's house? ¹⁵Are we not counted of him strangers? For he hath sold us, and hath quite

devoured also our money. ¹⁶ For all the riches which God hath taken from our father, that is ours, and our children's; now then, whatsoever God hath said unto thee, do.'

¹⁷ Then Jacob rose up, and set his sons and his wives upon camels; ¹⁸ and he carried away all his cattle, and all his goods which he had gotten, the cattle of his getting, which he had gotten in Padan-aram, for to go to Isaac his father in the land of Canaan. ¹⁹ And Laban went to shear his sheep: and Rachel had stolen the images that were her father's. ²⁰ And Jacob stole away unawares to Laban the Syrian, in that he told him not that he fled. ²¹ So he fled with all that he had; and he rose up, and passed over the river, and set his face toward the mount Gilead. ²² And it was told Laban on the third day that Jacob was fled. ²³ And he took his brethren with him, and pursued after him seven days' journey; and they overtook him in the mount Gilead. ²⁴ And God came to Laban the Syrian in a dream by night, and said unto him, 'Take heed that thou speak not to Jacob either good or bad.'

²⁵ Then Laban overtook Jacob. Now Jacob had pitched his tent in the mount; and Laban with his brethren pitched in the mount of Gilead. ²⁶ And Laban said to Jacob, 'What hast thou done, that thou hast stolen away unawares to me, and carried away my daughters, as captives taken with the sword? ²⁷ Wherefore didst thou flee away secretly, and steal away from me; and didst not tell me, that I might have sent thee away with mirth, and with songs, with tabret, and with harp? ²⁸ And hast not suffered me to kiss my sons and my daughters? Thou hast now done foolishly in so doing. ²⁹ It is

in the power of my hand to do you hurt; but the God of your father spake unto me yesternight, saying, "Take thou heed that thou speak not to Jacob either good or bad." ³⁰And now, though thou wouldest needs be gone, because thou sore long-edst after thy father's house, yet wherefore hast thou stolen my gods?' ³¹And Jacob answered and said to Laban, 'Because I was afraid: for I said, peradventure thou wouldest take by force thy daughters from me. ³²With whomsoever thou find-est thy gods, let him not live; before our brethren discern thou what is thine with me, and take it to thee.' For Jacob knew not that Rachel had stolen them. ³³And Laban went into Jacob's tent, and into Leah's tent, and into the two maid-servants' tents; but he found them not. Then went he out of Leah's tent, and entered into Rachel's tent. ³⁴Now Rachel had taken the images, and put them in the camel's furniture, and sat upon them. And Laban searched all the tent, but found them not. ³⁵And she said to her father, 'Let it not dis-please my lord that I cannot rise up before thee; for the cus-tom of women is upon me.' And he searched, but found not the images.

³⁶And Jacob was wroth, and chode with Laban; and Jacob answered and said to Laban, 'What is my trespass? What is my sin, that thou hast so hotly pursued after me? ³⁷Whereas thou hast searched all my stuff, what hast thou found of all thy household stuff? Set it here before my brethren and thy brethren, that they may judge betwixt us both. ³⁸This twenty years have I been with thee; thy ewes and thy she goats have not cast their young, and the rams of thy flock have I not

eaten. ³⁹ That which was torn of beasts I brought not unto thee; I bare the loss of it; of my hand didst thou require it, whether stolen by day, or stolen by night. ⁴⁰ Thus I was; in the day the drought consumed me, and the frost by night; and my sleep departed from mine eyes. ⁴¹ Thus have I been twenty years in thy house; I served thee fourteen years for thy two daughters, and six years for thy cattle; and thou hast changed my wages ten times. ⁴² Except the God of my father, the God of Abraham, and the fear of Isaac, had been with me, surely thou hadst sent me away now empty. God hath seen mine affliction and the labour of my hands, and rebuked thee yesternight.'

⁴³ And Laban answered and said unto Jacob, 'These daughters are my daughters, and these children are my children, and these cattle are my cattle, and all that thou seest is mine; and what can I do this day unto these my daughters, or unto their children which they have born? ⁴⁴ Now therefore come thou, let us make a covenant, I and thou; and let it be for a witness between me and thee.' ⁴⁵ And Jacob took a stone, and set it up for a pillar. ⁴⁶ And Jacob said unto his brethren, 'Gather stones'; and they took stones, and made an heap; and they did eat there upon the heap. ⁴⁷ And Laban called it Jegar-sahadutha; but Jacob called it Galeed. ⁴⁸ And Laban said, 'This heap is a witness between me and thee this day.' Therefore was the name of it called Galeed; ⁴⁹ and Mizpah; for he said, 'The Lord watch between me and thee, when we are absent one from another. ⁵⁰ If thou shalt afflict my daughters, or if thou shalt take other wives beside my daughters, no man is

with us; see, God is witness betwixt me and thee.' ⁵¹And Laban said to Jacob, 'Behold this heap, and behold this pillar, which I have cast betwixt me and thee; ⁵²this heap be witness, and this pillar be witness, that I will not pass over this heap to thee, and that thou shalt not pass over this heap and this pillar unto me, for harm. ⁵³The God of Abraham, and the God of Nahor, the God of their father, judge betwixt us.' And Jacob sware by the fear of his father Isaac. ⁵⁴Then Jacob offered sacrifice upon the mount, and called his brethren to eat bread; and they did eat bread, and tarried all night in the mount. ⁵⁵And early in the morning Laban rose up, and kissed his sons and his daughters, and blessed them; and Laban departed, and returned unto his place.

32 And Jacob went on his way, and the angels of God met him. ²And when Jacob saw them, he said, 'This is God's host,' and he called the name of that place Mahanaim. ³And Jacob sent messengers before him to Esau his brother unto the land of Seir, the country of Edom. ⁴And he commanded them, saying, 'Thus shall ye speak unto my lord Esau: thy servant Jacob saith thus, I have sojourned with Laban, and stayed there until now; ⁵and I have oxen, and asses, flocks, and menservants, and womenservants: and I have sent to tell my lord, that I may find grace in thy sight.'

⁶And the messengers returned to Jacob, saying, 'We came to thy brother Esau, and also he cometh to meet thee, and four hundred men with him.' ⁷Then Jacob was greatly afraid and distressed; and he divided the people that was

with him, and the flocks, and herds, and the camels, into two bands; ⁸and said, 'If Esau come to the one company, and smite it, then the other company which is left shall escape.'

⁹And Jacob said, 'O God of my father Abraham, and God of my father Isaac, the Lord which saidst unto me, "Return unto thy country, and to thy kindred, and I will deal well with thee"; ¹⁰I am not worthy of the least of all the mercies, and of all the truth, which thou hast shewed unto thy servant; for with my staff I passed over this Jordan; and now I am become two bands. ¹¹Deliver me, I pray thee, from the hand of my brother, from the hand of Esau; for I fear him, lest he will come and smite me, and the mother with the children. ¹²And thou saidst, "I will surely do thee good, and make thy seed as the sand of the sea, which cannot be numbered for multitude."'

¹³And he lodged there that same night; and took of that which came to his hand a present for Esau his brother: ¹⁴two hundred she goats, and twenty he goats, two hundred ewes, and twenty rams, ¹⁵thirty milch camels with their colts, forty kine, and ten bulls, twenty she asses, and ten foals. ¹⁶And he delivered them into the hand of his servants, every drove by themselves; and said unto his servants, 'Pass over before me, and put a space betwixt drove and drove.' ¹⁷And he commanded the foremost, saying, 'When Esau my brother meeteth thee, and asketh thee, saying, "Whose art thou? And whither goest thou? And whose are these before thee?" ¹⁸Then thou shalt say, "They be thy servant Jacob's; it is a present sent unto my lord Esau; and, behold, also he is behind us."' ¹⁹And

so commanded he the second, and the third, and all that followed the droves, saying, 'On this manner shall ye speak unto Esau, when ye find him. ²⁰And say ye moreover, "Behold, thy servant Jacob is behind us."' For he said, 'I will appease him with the present that goeth before me, and afterward I will see his face; peradventure he will accept of me.' ²¹So went the present over before him; and himself lodged that night in the company. ²²And he rose up that night, and took his two wives, and his two womenservants, and his eleven sons, and passed over the ford Jabbok. ²³And he took them, and sent them over the brook, and sent over that he had.

²⁴And Jacob was left alone; and there wrestled a man with him until the breaking of the day. ²⁵And when he saw that he prevailed not against him, he touched the hollow of his thigh; and the hollow of Jacob's thigh was out of joint, as he wrestled with him. ²⁶And the man said, 'Let me go, for the day breaketh.' And Jacob said, 'I will not let thee go, except thou bless me.' ²⁷And the man said unto him, 'What is thy name?' And he said, 'Jacob.' ²⁸And the man said, 'Thy name shall be called no more Jacob, but Israel; for as a prince hast thou power with God and with men, and hast prevailed.' ²⁹And Jacob asked him, and said, 'Tell me, I pray thee, thy name.' And he said, 'Wherefore is it that thou dost ask after my name?' And he blessed him there. ³⁰And Jacob called the name of the place Peniel; 'for I have seen God face to face, and my life is preserved'. ³¹And as he passed over Penuel the sun rose upon him, and he halted upon his thigh. ³²Therefore the children of Israel eat not of the sinew which shrank,

which is upon the hollow of the thigh, unto this day: because he touched the hollow of Jacob's thigh in the sinew that shrank.

33 And Jacob lifted up his eyes, and looked, and, behold, Esau came, and with him four hundred men. And he divided the children unto Leah, and unto Rachel, and unto the two handmaids. ²And he put the handmaids and their children foremost, and Leah and her children after, and Rachel and Joseph hindermost. ³And he passed over before them, and bowed himself to the ground seven times, until he came near to his brother. ⁴And Esau ran to meet him, and embraced him, and fell on his neck, and kissed him; and they wept. ⁵And he lifted up his eyes, and saw the women and the children; and said, 'Who are those with thee?' And Jacob said, 'The children which God hath graciously given thy servant.' ⁶Then the handmaidens came near, they and their children, and they bowed themselves. ⁷And Leah also with her children came near, and bowed themselves; and after came Joseph near and Rachel, and they bowed themselves. ⁸And Esau said, 'What meanest thou by all this drove which I met?' And Jacob said, 'These are to find grace in the sight of my lord.' ⁹And Esau said, 'I have enough, my brother; keep that thou hast unto thyself.' ¹⁰And Jacob said, 'Nay, I pray thee, if now I have found grace in thy sight, then receive my present at my hand; for therefore I have seen thy face, as though I had seen the face of God, and thou wast pleased with me. ¹¹Take, I pray thee, my blessing that is brought to thee; because God hath dealt graciously with me, and because I have enough.' And he urged him, and he took it. ¹²And Esau said, 'Let us take our journey, and let us go, and I will go before thee.' ¹³And Jacob said unto him, 'My lord knoweth that the children are tender, and the flocks and herds with young are with me; and if men should overdrive them one day, all the flock will die. ¹⁴Let my lord, I pray thee, pass over before his servant: and I will lead on softly, according as the cattle that goeth before me and the children be able to endure, until I come unto my lord unto Seir.' ¹⁵And Esau said, 'Let me now leave with thee some of the folk that are with me.' And he said, 'What needeth it? Let me find grace in the sight of my lord.'

¹⁶So Esau returned that day on his way unto Seir. ¹⁷And Jacob journeyed to Succoth, and built him an house, and made booths for his cattle; therefore the name of the place is called Succoth.

¹⁸And Jacob came to Shalem, a city of Shechem, which is in the land of Canaan, when he came from Padan-aram; and pitched his tent before the city. ¹⁹And he bought a parcel of a field, where he had spread his tent, at the hand of the children of Hamor, Shechem's father, for an hundred pieces of money. ²⁰And he erected there an altar, and called it El-elohe-Israel.

34 And Dinah the daughter of Leah, which she bare unto Jacob, went out to see the daughters of the land. ²And when Shechem the son of Hamor the Hivite, prince of the country, saw her, he took her, and lay with her, and

defiled her. ³And his soul clave unto Dinah the daughter of Jacob, and he loved the damsel, and spake kindly unto the damsel. ⁴And Shechem spake unto his father Hamor, saying, 'Get me this damsel to wife.' ⁵And Jacob heard that he had defiled Dinah his daughter; now his sons were with his cattle in the field: and Jacob held his peace until they were come.

⁶And Hamor the father of Shechem went out unto Jacob to commune with him. ⁷And the sons of Jacob came out of the field when they heard it: and the men were grieved, and they were very wroth, because he had wrought folly in Israel in lying with Jacob's daughter; which thing ought not to be done. ⁸And Hamor communed with them, saying, 'The soul of my son Shechem longeth for your daughter; I pray you give her him to wife. ⁹And make ye marriages with us, and give your daughters unto us, and take our daughters unto you. ¹⁰And ye shall dwell with us; and the land shall be before you; dwell and trade ye therein, and get you possessions therein.' ¹¹And Shechem said unto her father and unto her brethren, 'Let me find grace in your eyes, and what ye shall say unto me I will give. ¹²Ask me never so much dowry and gift, and I will give according as ye shall say unto me; but give me the damsel to wife.' ¹³And the sons of Jacob answered Shechem and Hamor his father deceitfully, and said, because he had defiled Dinah their sister: ¹⁴and they said unto them, 'We cannot do this thing, to give our sister to one that is uncircumcised; for that were a reproach unto us; ¹⁵but in this will we consent unto you: if ye will be as we be, that every male of you be circumcised; ¹⁶then will we give

our daughters unto you, and we will take your daughters to us, and we will dwell with you, and we will become one people. ¹⁷But if ye will not hearken unto us, to be circumcised; then will we take our daughter, and we will be gone.' ¹⁸And their words pleased Hamor, and Shechem Hamor's son. ¹⁹And the young man deferred not to do the thing, because he had delight in Jacob's daughter; and he was more honourable than all the house of his father.

²⁰And Hamor and Shechem his son came unto the gate of their city, and communed with the men of their city, saying, ²¹'These men are peaceable with us; therefore let them dwell in the land, and trade therein; for the land, behold, it is large enough for them; let us take their daughters to us for wives, and let us give them our daughters. ²²Only herein will the men consent unto us for to dwell with us, to be one people, if every male among us be circumcised, as they are circumcised. ²³Shall not their cattle and their substance and every beast of theirs be ours? Only let us consent unto them, and they will dwell with us.' ²⁴And unto Hamor and unto Shechem his son hearkened all that went out of the gate of his city; and every male was circumcised, all that went out of the gate of his city.

²⁵And it came to pass on the third day, when they were sore, that two of the sons of Jacob, Simeon and Levi, Dinah's brethren, took each man his sword, and came upon the city boldly, and slew all the males. ²⁶And they slew Hamor and Shechem his son with the edge of the sword, and took Dinah out of Shechem's house, and went out. ²⁷The sons of Jacob

came upon the slain, and spoiled the city, because they had defiled their sister. ²⁸ They took their sheep, and their oxen, and their asses, and that which was in the city, and that which was in the field, ²⁹ and all their wealth, and all their little ones, and their wives took they captive, and spoiled even all that was in the house. ³⁰And Jacob said to Simeon and Levi, 'Ye have troubled me to make me to stink among the inhabitants of the land, among the Canaanites and the Perizzites; and I being few in number, they shall gather themselves together against me, and slay me; and I shall be destroyed, I and my house.' ³¹And they said, 'Should he deal with our sister as with an harlot?'

35 And God said unto Jacob, 'Arise, go up to Beth-el, and dwell there; and make there an altar unto God, that appeared unto thee when thou fleddest from the face of Esau thy brother.' ² Then Jacob said unto his household, and to all that were with him, 'Put away the strange gods that are among you, and be clean, and change your garments; ³ and let us arise, and go up to Beth-el; and I will make there an altar unto God, who answered me in the day of my distress, and was with me in the way which I went.' ⁴And they gave unto Jacob all the strange gods which were in their hand, and all their earrings which were in their ears; and Jacob hid them under the oak which was by Shechem. ⁵And they journeyed; and the terror of God was upon the cities that were round about them, and they did not pursue after the sons of Jacob.

⁶ So Jacob came to Luz, which is in the land of Canaan,

that is, Beth-el, he and all the people that were with him. [7]And he built there an altar, and called the place El-beth-el; because there God appeared unto him, when he fled from the face of his brother. [8]But Deborah Rebekah's nurse died, and she was buried beneath Beth-el under an oak; and the name of it was called Allon-bachuth.

[9]And God appeared unto Jacob again, when he came out of Padan-aram, and blessed him. [10]And God said unto him, 'Thy name is Jacob: thy name shall not be called any more Jacob, but Israel shall be thy name,' and he called his name Israel. [11]And God said unto him, 'I am God Almighty: be fruitful and multiply; a nation and a company of nations shall be of thee, and kings shall come out of thy loins; [12]and the land which I gave Abraham and Isaac, to thee I will give it, and to thy seed after thee will I give the land.' [13]And God went up from him in the place where he talked with him. [14]And Jacob set up a pillar in the place where he talked with him, even a pillar of stone; and he poured a drink offering thereon, and he poured oil thereon. [15]And Jacob called the name of the place where God spake with him, Beth-el.

[16]And they journeyed from Beth-el; and there was but a little way to come to Ephrath; and Rachel travailed, and she had hard labour. [17]And it came to pass, when she was in hard labour, that the midwife said unto her, 'Fear not; thou shalt have this son also.' [18]And it came to pass, as her soul was in departing (for she died) that she called his name Ben-oni; but his father called him Benjamin. [19]And Rachel died, and was buried in the way to Ephrath, which is Bethlehem. [20]And

Jacob set a pillar upon her grave; that is the pillar of Rachel's grave unto this day.

²¹And Israel journeyed, and spread his tent beyond the tower of Edar. ²²And it came to pass, when Israel dwelt in that land, that Reuben went and lay with Bilhah his father's concubine; and Israel heard it. Now the sons of Jacob were twelve. ²³The sons of Leah: Reuben, Jacob's firstborn, and Simeon, and Levi, and Judah, and Issachar, and Zebulun; ²⁴the sons of Rachel: Joseph, and Benjamin; ²⁵and the sons of Bilhah, Rachel's handmaid: Dan, and Naphtali; ²⁶and the sons of Zilpah, Leah's handmaid: Gad, and Asher: these are the sons of Jacob, which were born to him in Padan-aram.

²⁷And Jacob came unto Isaac his father unto Mamre, unto the city of Arbah, which is Hebron, where Abraham and Isaac sojourned. ²⁸And the days of Isaac were an hundred and fourscore years. ²⁹And Isaac gave up the ghost, and died, and was gathered unto his people, being old and full of days; and his sons Esau and Jacob buried him.

36 Now these are the generations of Esau, who is Edom. ²Esau took his wives of the daughters of Canaan; Adah the daughter of Elon the Hittite, and Aholibamah the daughter of Anah the daughter of Zibeon the Hivite; ³and Bashemath Ishmael's daughter, sister of Nebajoth. ⁴And Adah bare to Esau Eliphaz; and Bashemath bare Reuel; ⁵and Aholibamah bare Jeush, and Jaalam, and Korah. These are the sons of Esau, which were born unto him in the land of Canaan. ⁶And Esau took his wives, and his sons, and his

daughters, and all the persons of his house, and his cattle, and all his beasts, and all his substance, which he had got in the land of Canaan; and went into the country from the face of his brother Jacob. ⁷For their riches were more than that they might dwell together; and the land wherein they were strangers could not bear them because of their cattle. ⁸Thus dwelt Esau in mount Seir: Esau is Edom.

⁹And these are the generations of Esau the father of the Edomites in mount Seir. ¹⁰These are the names of Esau's sons: Eliphaz the son of Adah the wife of Esau, Reuel the son of Bashemath the wife of Esau. ¹¹And the sons of Eliphaz were Teman, Omar, Zepho, and Gatam, and Kenaz. ¹²And Timna was concubine to Eliphaz Esau's son; and she bare to Eliphaz Amalek. These were the sons of Adah Esau's wife. ¹³And these are the sons of Reuel: Nahath, and Zerah, Shammah, and Mizzah. These were the sons of Bashemath Esau's wife.

¹⁴And these were the sons of Aholibamah, the daughter of Anah the daughter of Zibeon, Esau's wife: and she bare to Esau Jeush, and Jaalam, and Korah.

¹⁵These were dukes of the sons of Esau; the sons of Eliphaz the firstborn son of Esau; duke Teman, duke Omar, duke Zepho, duke Kenaz, ¹⁶duke Korah, duke Gatam, and duke Amalek: these are the dukes that came of Eliphaz in the land of Edom. These were the sons of Adah.

¹⁷And these are the sons of Reuel Esau's son: duke Nahath, duke Zerah, duke Shammah, duke Mizzah. These are the dukes that came of Reuel in the land of Edom; these are the sons of Bashemath Esau's wife.

¹⁸And these are the sons of Aholibamah Esau's wife: duke Jeush, duke Jaalam, duke Korah. These were the dukes that came of Aholibamah the daughter of Anah, Esau's wife. ¹⁹These are the sons of Esau, who is Edom, and these are their dukes.

²⁰These are the sons of Seir the Horite, who inhabited the land: Lotan, and Shobal, and Zibeon, and Anah, ²¹and Dishon, and Ezer, and Dishan. These are the dukes of the Horites, the children of Seir in the land of Edom. ²²And the children of Lotan were Hori and Hemam; and Lotan's sister was Timna. ²³And the children of Shobal were these: Alvan, and Manahath, and Ebal, Shepho, and Onam. ²⁴And these are the children of Zibeon: both Ajah, and Anah. This was that Anah that found the mules in the wilderness, as he fed the asses of Zibeon his father. ²⁵And the children of Anah were these: Dishon, and Aholibamah the daughter of Anah. ²⁶And these are the children of Dishon: Hemdan, and Eshban, and Ithran, and Cheran. ²⁷The children of Ezer are these: Bilhan, and Zaavan, and Akan. ²⁸The children of Dishan are these: Uz, and Aran. ²⁹These are the dukes that came of the Horites: duke Lotan, duke Shobal, duke Zibeon, duke Anah, ³⁰duke Dishon, duke Ezer, duke Dishan. These are the dukes that came of Hori, among their dukes in the land of Seir.

³¹And these are the kings that reigned in the land of Edom, before there reigned any king over the children of Israel. ³²And Bela the son of Beor reigned in Edom; and the name of his city was Dinhabah. ³³And Bela died, and Jobab the son of Zerah of Bozrah reigned in his stead. ³⁴And Jobab died, and Husham of the land of Temani reigned in his stead. ³⁵And

Husham died, and Hadad the son of Bedad, who smote Midian in the field of Moab, reigned in his stead; and the name of his city was Avith. ³⁶And Hadad died, and Samlah of Masrekah reigned in his stead. ³⁷And Samlah died, and Saul of Rehoboth by the river reigned in his stead. ³⁸And Saul died, and Baal-hanan the son of Achbor reigned in his stead. ³⁹And Baal-hanan the son of Achbor died, and Hadar reigned in his stead: and the name of his city was Pau; and his wife's name was Mehetabel, the daughter of Matred, the daughter of Mezahab. ⁴⁰And these are the names of the dukes that came of Esau, according to their families, after their places, by their names: duke Timnah, duke Alvah, duke Jetheth, ⁴¹duke Aholibamah, duke Elah, duke Pinon, ⁴²duke Kenaz, duke Teman, duke Mibzar, ⁴³duke Magdiel, duke Iram. These be the dukes of Edom, according to their habitations in the land of their possession; he is Esau the father of the Edomites.

37 And Jacob dwelt in the land wherein his father was a stranger, in the land of Canaan. ² These are the generations of Jacob. Joseph, being seventeen years old, was feeding the flock with his brethren; and the lad was with the sons of Bilhah, and with the sons of Zilpah, his father's wives; and Joseph brought unto his father their evil report. ³ Now Israel loved Joseph more than all his children, because he was the son of his old age; and he made him a coat of many colours. ⁴And when his brethren saw that their father loved him more than all his brethren, they hated him, and could not speak peaceably unto him.

⁵And Joseph dreamed a dream, and he told it his brethren; and they hated him yet the more. ⁶And he said unto them, 'Hear, I pray you, this dream which I have dreamed: ⁷for, behold, we were binding sheaves in the field, and, lo, my sheaf arose, and also stood upright; and, behold, your sheaves stood round about, and made obeisance to my sheaf.' ⁸And his brethren said to him, 'Shalt thou indeed reign over us? Or shalt thou indeed have dominion over us?' And they hated him yet the more for his dreams, and for his words.

⁹And he dreamed yet another dream, and told it his brethren, and said, 'Behold, I have dreamed a dream more; and, behold, the sun and the moon and the eleven stars made obeisance to me.' ¹⁰And he told it to his father, and to his brethren; and his father rebuked him, and said unto him, 'What is this dream that thou hast dreamed? Shall I and thy mother and thy brethren indeed come to bow down ourselves to thee to the earth?' ¹¹And his brethren envied him; but his father observed the saying.

¹²And his brethren went to feed their father's flock in Shechem. ¹³And Israel said unto Joseph, 'Do not thy brethren feed the flock in Shechem? Come, and I will send thee unto them.' And he said to him, 'Here am I.' ¹⁴And he said to him, 'Go, I pray thee, see whether it be well with thy brethren, and well with the flocks; and bring me word again.' So he sent him out of the vale of Hebron, and he came to Shechem.

¹⁵And a certain man found him, and, behold, he was wandering in the field; and the man asked him, saying, 'What seekest thou?' ¹⁶And he said, 'I seek my brethren; tell me, I

pray thee, where they feed their flocks.' ¹⁷And the man said, 'They are departed hence; for I heard them say, "Let us go to Dothan."' And Joseph went after his brethren, and found them in Dothan. ¹⁸And when they saw him afar off, even before he came near unto them, they conspired against him to slay him. ¹⁹And they said one to another, 'Behold, this dreamer cometh. ²⁰ Come now therefore, and let us slay him, and cast him into some pit, and we will say, "Some evil beast hath devoured him;" and we shall see what will become of his dreams.' ²¹And Reuben heard it, and he delivered him out of their hands; and said, 'Let us not kill him.' ²²And Reuben said unto them, 'Shed no blood, but cast him into this pit that is in the wilderness, and lay no hand upon him,' that he might rid him out of their hands, to deliver him to his father again.

²³And it came to pass, when Joseph was come unto his brethren, that they stript Joseph out of his coat, his coat of many colours that was on him; ²⁴ and they took him, and cast him into a pit; and the pit was empty, there was no water in it. ²⁵And they sat down to eat bread; and they lifted up their eyes and looked, and, behold, a company of Ishmeelites came from Gilead with their camels bearing spicery and balm and myrrh, going to carry it down to Egypt. ²⁶And Judah said unto his brethren, 'What profit is it if we slay our brother, and conceal his blood? ²⁷Come, and let us sell him to the Ishmeelites, and let not our hand be upon him; for he is our brother and our flesh.' And his brethren were content. ²⁸ Then there passed by Midianite merchantmen; and they drew and lifted up Joseph out of the pit, and sold Joseph to the

Ishmeelites for twenty pieces of silver; and they brought Joseph into Egypt.

²⁹And Reuben returned unto the pit; and, behold, Joseph was not in the pit; and he rent his clothes. ³⁰And he returned unto his brethren, and said, 'The child is not; and I, whither shall I go?' ³¹And they took Joseph's coat, and killed a kid of the goats, and dipped the coat in the blood; ³²and they sent the coat of many colours, and they brought it to their father; and said, 'This have we found: know now whether it be thy son's coat or no.' ³³And he knew it, and said, 'It is my son's coat; an evil beast hath devoured him; Joseph is without doubt rent in pieces.' ³⁴And Jacob rent his clothes, and put sackcloth upon his loins, and mourned for his son many days. ³⁵And all his sons and all his daughters rose up to comfort him; but he refused to be comforted; and he said, 'For I will go down into the grave unto my son mourning.' Thus his father wept for him. ³⁶And the Midianites sold him into Egypt unto Potiphar, an officer of Pharaoh's, and captain of the guard.

38 And it came to pass at that time that Judah went down from his brethren, and turned in to a certain Adullamite, whose name was Hirah. ²And Judah saw there a daughter of a certain Canaanite, whose name was Shuah; and he took her, and went in unto her. ³And she conceived, and bare a son; and he called his name Er. ⁴And she conceived again, and bare a son; and she called his name Onan. ⁵And she yet again conceived, and bare a son; and called his

name Shelah; and he was at Chezib, when she bare him.
⁶And Judah took a wife for Er his firstborn, whose name was
Tamar. ⁷And Er, Judah's firstborn, was wicked in the sight of
the Lord; and the Lord slew him. ⁸And Judah said unto Onan,
'Go in unto thy brother's wife, and marry her, and raise up
seed to thy brother.' ⁹And Onan knew that the seed should
not be his; and it came to pass, when he went in unto his
brother's wife, that he spilled it on the ground, lest that he
should give seed to his brother. ¹⁰And the thing which he did
displeased the Lord; wherefore he slew him also. ¹¹Then said
Judah to Tamar his daughter in law, 'Remain a widow at thy
father's house, till Shelah my son be grown,' for he said, 'lest
peradventure he die also, as his brethren did.' And Tamar
went and dwelt in her father's house.

   ¹²And in process of time the daughter of Shuah Judah's
wife died; and Judah was comforted, and went up unto his
sheepshearers to Timnath, he and his friend Hirah the Adullamite. ¹³And it was told Tamar, saying, 'Behold thy father in
law goeth up to Timnath to shear his sheep.' ¹⁴And she put
her widow's garments off from her, and covered her with a
vail, and wrapped herself, and sat in an open place, which is
by the way to Timnath; for she saw that Shelah was grown,
and she was not given unto him to wife. ¹⁵When Judah saw
her, he thought her to be an harlot; because she had covered
her face. ¹⁶And he turned unto her by the way, and said, 'Go
to, I pray thee, let me come in unto thee' (for he knew not
that she was his daughter in law). And she said, 'What wilt
thou give me, that thou mayest come in unto me?' ¹⁷And he

said, 'I will send thee a kid from the flock.' And she said, 'Wilt thou give me a pledge, till thou send it?' ¹⁸And he said, 'What pledge shall I give thee?' And she said, 'Thy signet, and thy bracelets, and thy staff that is in thine hand.' And he gave it her, and came in unto her, and she conceived by him. ¹⁹And she arose, and went away, and laid by her vail from her, and put on the garments of her widowhood. ²⁰And Judah sent the kid by the hand of his friend the Adullamite, to receive his pledge from the woman's hand: but he found her not. ²¹Then he asked the men of that place, saying, 'Where is the harlot, that was openly by the way side?' And they said, 'There was no harlot in this place.' ²²And he returned to Judah, and said, 'I cannot find her; and also the men of the place said, that there was no harlot in this place.' ²³And Judah said, 'Let her take it to her, lest we be shamed; behold, I sent this kid, and thou hast not found her.'

²⁴And it came to pass about three months after, that it was told Judah, saying, 'Tamar thy daughter in law hath played the harlot; and also, behold, she is with child by whoredom.' And Judah said, 'Bring her forth, and let her be burnt.' ²⁵ When she was brought forth, she sent to her father in law, saying, 'By the man, whose these are, am I with child,' and she said, 'Discern, I pray thee, whose are these, the signet, and bracelets, and staff.' ²⁶And Judah acknowledged them, and said, 'She hath been more righteous than I; because that I gave her not to Shelah my son.' And he knew her again no more.

²⁷And it came to pass in the time of her travail, that, behold, twins were in her womb. ²⁸And it came to pass, when she

travailed, that the one put out his hand: and the midwife took and bound upon his hand a scarlet thread, saying, 'This came out first.' ²⁹And it came to pass, as he drew back his hand, that, behold, his brother came out; and she said, 'How hast thou broken forth? This breach be upon thee'; therefore his name was called Pharez. ³⁰And afterward came out his brother, that had the scarlet thread upon his hand; and his name was called Zarah.

39 And Joseph was brought down to Egypt; and Potiphar, an officer of Pharaoh, captain of the guard, an Egyptian, bought him of the hands of the Ishmeelites, which had brought him down thither. ²And the Lord was with Joseph, and he was a prosperous man; and he was in the house of his master the Egyptian. ³And his master saw that the Lord was with him, and that the Lord made all that he did to prosper in his hand. ⁴And Joseph found grace in his sight, and he served him; and he made him overseer over his house, and all that he had he put into his hand. ⁵And it came to pass from the time that he had made him overseer in his house, and over all that he had, that the Lord blessed the Egyptian's house for Joseph's sake; and the blessing of the Lord was upon all that he had in the house, and in the field. ⁶And he left all that he had in Joseph's hand; and he knew not ought he had, save the bread which he did eat. And Joseph was a goodly person, and well favoured.

⁷And it came to pass after these things that his master's wife cast her eyes upon Joseph; and she said, 'Lie with me.'

⁸ But he refused, and said unto his master's wife, 'Behold, my master wotteth not what is with me in the house, and he hath committed all that he hath to my hand; ⁹ there is none greater in this house than I; neither hath he kept back any thing from me but thee, because thou art his wife; how then can I do this great wickedness, and sin against God?' ¹⁰And it came to pass, as she spake to Joseph day by day, that he hearkened not unto her, to lie by her, or to be with her. ¹¹And it came to pass about this time, that Joseph went into the house to do his business; and there was none of the men of the house there within. ¹²And she caught him by his garment, saying, 'Lie with me'; and he left his garment in her hand, and fled, and got him out. ¹³And it came to pass, when she saw that he had left his garment in her hand, and was fled forth, ¹⁴ that she called unto the men of her house, and spake unto them, saying, 'See, he hath brought in an Hebrew unto us to mock us; he came in unto me to lie with me, and I cried with a loud voice; ¹⁵ and it came to pass, when he heard that I lifted up my voice and cried, that he left his garment with me, and fled, and got him out.' ¹⁶And she laid up his garment by her, until his lord came home. ¹⁷And she spake unto him according to these words, saying, 'The Hebrew servant, which thou hast brought unto us, came in unto me to mock me; ¹⁸ and it came to pass, as I lifted up my voice and cried, that he left his garment with me, and fled out.' ¹⁹And it came to pass, when his master heard the words of his wife, which she spake unto him, saying, 'After this manner did thy servant to me,' that his wrath was kindled. ²⁰And Joseph's master

took him, and put him into the prison, a place where the king's prisoners were bound; and he was there in the prison.

²¹ But the Lord was with Joseph, and shewed him mercy, and gave him favour in the sight of the keeper of the prison. ²² And the keeper of the prison committed to Joseph's hand all the prisoners that were in the prison; and whatsoever they did there, he was the doer of it. ²³ The keeper of the prison looked not to any thing that was under his hand; because the Lord was with him, and that which he did, the Lord made it to prosper.

40 And it came to pass after these things, that the butler of the king of Egypt and his baker had offended their lord the king of Egypt. ²And Pharaoh was wroth against two of his officers, against the chief of the butlers, and against the chief of the bakers. ³And he put them in ward in the house of the captain of the guard, into the prison, the place where Joseph was bound. ⁴And the captain of the guard charged Joseph with them, and he served them; and they continued a season in ward.

⁵And they dreamed a dream both of them, each man his dream in one night, each man according to the interpretation of his dream, the butler and the baker of the king of Egypt, which were bound in the prison. ⁶And Joseph came in unto them in the morning, and looked upon them, and, behold, they were sad. ⁷And he asked Pharaoh's officers that were with him in the ward of his lord's house, saying, 'Wherefore look ye so sadly to day?' ⁸And they said unto him, 'We have

dreamed a dream, and there is no interpreter of it.' And Joseph said unto them, 'Do not interpretations belong to God? Tell me them, I pray you.' ⁹And the chief butler told his dream to Joseph, and said to him, 'In my dream, behold, a vine was before me; ¹⁰and in the vine were three branches: and it was as though it budded, and her blossoms shot forth; and the clusters thereof brought forth ripe grapes; ¹¹and Pharaoh's cup was in my hand; and I took the grapes, and pressed them into Pharaoh's cup, and I gave the cup into Pharaoh's hand.' ¹²And Joseph said unto him, 'This is the interpretation of it. The three branches are three days; ¹³yet within three days shall Pharaoh lift up thine head, and restore thee unto thy place; and thou shalt deliver Pharaoh's cup into his hand, after the former manner when thou wast his butler. ¹⁴But think on me when it shall be well with thee, and shew kindness, I pray thee, unto me, and make mention of me unto Pharaoh, and bring me out of this house; ¹⁵for indeed I was stolen away out of the land of the Hebrews; and here also have I done nothing that they should put me into the dungeon.'

¹⁶When the chief baker saw that the interpretation was good, he said unto Joseph, 'I also was in my dream, and, behold, I had three white baskets on my head; ¹⁷and in the uppermost basket there was of all manner of bakemeats for Pharaoh; and the birds did eat them out of the basket upon my head.' ¹⁸And Joseph answered and said, 'This is the interpretation thereof. The three baskets are three days; ¹⁹yet within three days shall Pharaoh lift up thy head from off thee, and shall hang thee on a tree; and the birds shall eat thy flesh from off thee.'

²⁰And it came to pass the third day, which was Pharaoh's birthday, that he made a feast unto all his servants; and he lifted up the head of the chief butler and of the chief baker among his servants. ²¹And he restored the chief butler unto his butlership again; and he gave the cup into Pharaoh's hand; ²² but he hanged the chief baker, as Joseph had interpreted to them. ²³ Yet did not the chief butler remember Joseph, but forgat him.

41 And it came to pass at the end of two full years, that Pharaoh dreamed; and, behold, he stood by the river. ²And, behold, there came up out of the river seven well favoured kine and fatfleshed; and they fed in a meadow. ³And, behold, seven other kine came up after them out of the river, ill favoured and leanfleshed; and stood by the other kine upon the brink of the river. ⁴And the ill favoured and leanfleshed kine did eat up the seven well favoured and fat kine. So Pharaoh awoke. ⁵And he slept and dreamed the second time; and, behold, seven ears of corn came up upon one stalk, rank and good. ⁶And, behold, seven thin ears and blasted with the east wind sprung up after them. ⁷And the seven thin ears devoured the seven rank and full ears. And Pharaoh awoke, and, behold, it was a dream. ⁸And it came to pass in the morning that his spirit was troubled; and he sent and called for all the magicians of Egypt, and all the wise men thereof; and Pharaoh told them his dream; but there was none that could interpret them unto Pharaoh.

⁹ Then spake the chief butler unto Pharaoh, saying, 'I do remember my faults this day: ¹⁰Pharaoh was wroth with his

servants, and put me in ward in the captain of the guard's house, both me and the chief baker; ¹¹and we dreamed a dream in one night, I and he; we dreamed each man according to the interpretation of his dream. ¹²And there was there with us a young man, an Hebrew, servant to the captain of the guard; and we told him, and he interpreted to us our dreams; to each man according to his dream he did interpret. ¹³And it came to pass, as he interpreted to us, so it was; me he restored unto mine office, and him he hanged.'

¹⁴Then Pharaoh sent and called Joseph, and they brought him hastily out of the dungeon; and he shaved himself, and changed his raiment, and came in unto Pharoah. ¹⁵And Pharaoh said unto Joseph, 'I have dreamed a dream, and there is none that can interpret it; and I have heard say of thee, that thou canst understand a dream to interpret it.' ¹⁶And Joseph answered Pharaoh, saying, 'It is not in me: God shall give Pharaoh an answer of peace.' ¹⁷And Pharaoh said unto Joseph, 'In my dream, behold, I stood upon the bank of the river; ¹⁸and, behold, there came up out of the river seven kine, fatfleshed and well favoured; and they fed in a meadow; ¹⁹and, behold, seven other kine came up after them, poor and very ill favoured and leanfleshed, such as I never saw in all the land of Egypt for badness; ²⁰and the lean and the ill favoured kine did eat up the first seven fat kine; ²¹and when they had eaten them up, it could not be known that they had eaten them; but they were still ill favoured, as at the beginning. So I awoke. ²²And I saw in my dream, and, behold, seven ears came up in one stalk, full and good; ²³and, behold, seven

ears, withered, thin, and blasted with the east wind, sprung up after them; ²⁴ and the thin ears devoured the seven good ears; and I told this unto the magicians; but there was none that could declare it to me.'

²⁵And Joseph said unto Pharaoh, 'The dream of Pharaoh is one: God hath shewed Pharaoh what he is about to do. ²⁶ The seven good kine are seven years; and the seven good ears are seven years: the dream is one. ²⁷And the seven thin and ill favoured kine that came up after them are seven years; and the seven empty ears blasted with the east wind shall be seven years of famine. ²⁸ This is the thing which I have spoken unto Pharaoh: what God is about to do he sheweth unto Pharaoh. ²⁹Behold, there come seven years of great plenty throughout all the land of Egypt; ³⁰ and there shall arise after them seven years of famine; and all the plenty shall be forgotten in the land of Egypt; and the famine shall consume the land; ³¹ and the plenty shall not be known in the land by reason of that famine following; for it shall be very grievous. ³²And for that the dream was doubled unto Pharaoh twice; it is because the thing is established by God, and God will shortly bring it to pass. ³³ Now therefore let Pharaoh look out a man discreet and wise, and set him over the land of Egypt. ³⁴ Let Pharaoh do this, and let him appoint officers over the land, and take up the fifth part of the land of Egypt in the seven plenteous years. ³⁵And let them gather all the food of those good years that come, and lay up corn under the hand of Pharaoh, and let them keep food in the cities. ³⁶And that food shall be for store to the land against the seven years of

famine, which shall be in the land of Egypt; that the land perish not through the famine.'

³⁷And the thing was good in the eyes of Pharaoh, and in the eyes of all his servants. ³⁸And Pharaoh said unto his servants, 'Can we find such a one as this is, a man in whom the Spirit of God is?' ³⁹And Pharaoh said unto Joseph, 'Forasmuch as God hath shewed thee all this, there is none so discreet and wise as thou art. ⁴⁰Thou shalt be over my house, and according unto thy word shall all my people be ruled; only in the throne will I be greater than thou.' ⁴¹And Pharaoh said unto Joseph, 'See, I have set thee over all the land of Egypt.' ⁴²And Pharaoh took off his ring from his hand, and put it upon Joseph's hand, and arrayed him in vestures of fine linen, and put a gold chain about his neck; ⁴³and he made him to ride in the second chariot which he had; and they cried before him, 'Bow the knee,' and he made him ruler over all the land of Egypt. ⁴⁴And Pharaoh said unto Joseph, 'I am Pharaoh, and without thee shall no man lift up his hand or foot in all the land of Egypt.' ⁴⁵And Pharaoh called Joseph's name Zaphnath-paaneah; and he gave him to wife Asenath the daughter of Potipherah priest of On. And Joseph went out over all the land of Egypt.

⁴⁶And Joseph was thirty years old when he stood before Pharaoh king of Egypt. And Joseph went out from the presence of Pharaoh, and went throughout all the land of Egypt. ⁴⁷And in the seven plenteous years the earth brought forth by handfuls. ⁴⁸And he gathered up all the food of the seven years, which were in the land of Egypt, and laid up the food

in the cities; the food of the field, which was round about every city, laid he up in the same. ⁴⁹And Joseph gathered corn as the sand of the sea, very much, until he left numbering; for it was without number. ⁵⁰And unto Joseph were born two sons before the years of famine came, which Asenath the daughter of Potipherah priest of On bare unto him. ⁵¹And Joseph called the name of the firstborn Manasseh: 'For God,' said he, 'hath made me forget all my toil, and all my father's house.' ⁵²And the name of the second called he Ephraim: 'For God hath caused me to be fruitful in the land of my affliction.'

⁵³And the seven years of plenteousness, that was in the land of Egypt, were ended. ⁵⁴And the seven years of dearth began to come, according as Joseph had said; and the dearth was in all lands; but in all the land of Egypt there was bread. ⁵⁵And when all the land of Egypt was famished, the people cried to Pharaoh for bread; and Pharaoh said unto all the Egyptians, 'Go unto Joseph; what he saith to you, do.' ⁵⁶And the famine was over all the face of the earth. And Joseph opened all the storehouses, and sold unto the Egyptians; and the famine waxed sore in the land of Egypt. ⁵⁷And all countries came into Egypt to Joseph for to buy corn; because that the famine was so sore in all lands.

42 Now when Jacob saw that there was corn in Egypt, Jacob said unto his sons, 'Why do ye look one upon another?' ²And he said, 'Behold, I have heard that there is corn in Egypt; get you down thither, and buy for us from thence; that we may live, and not die.'

³And Joseph's ten brethren went down to buy corn in Egypt. ⁴But Benjamin, Joseph's brother, Jacob sent not with his brethren; for he said, 'Lest peradventure mischief befall him.' ⁵And the sons of Israel came to buy corn among those that came; for the famine was in the land of Canaan. ⁶And Joseph was the governor over the land, and he it was that sold to all the people of the land; and Joseph's brethren came, and bowed down themselves before him with their faces to the earth. ⁷And Joseph saw his brethren, and he knew them, but made himself strange unto them, and spake roughly unto them; and he said unto them, 'Whence come ye?' And they said, 'From the land of Canaan to buy food.' ⁸And Joseph knew his brethren, but they knew not him. ⁹And Joseph remembered the dreams which he dreamed of them, and said unto them, 'Ye are spies; to see the nakedness of the land ye are come.' ¹⁰And they said unto him, 'Nay, my lord, but to buy food are thy servants come. ¹¹We are all one man's sons; we are true men, thy servants are no spies.' ¹²And he said unto them, 'Nay, but to see the nakedness of the land ye are come.' ¹³And they said, 'Thy servants are twelve brethren, the sons of one man in the land of Canaan; and, behold, the youngest is this day with our father, and one is not.' ¹⁴And Joseph said unto them, 'That is it that I spake unto you, saying, "Ye are spies"; ¹⁵hereby ye shall be proved: by the life of Pharaoh ye shall not go forth hence, except your youngest brother come hither. ¹⁶Send one of you, and let him fetch your brother, and ye shall be kept in prison, that your words may be proved, whether there be any truth in you; or else by the life of Pharaoh

surely ye are spies.' ¹⁷And he put them all together into ward three days.

¹⁸And Joseph said unto them the third day, 'This do, and live; for I fear God: ¹⁹if ye be true men, let one of your brethren be bound in the house of your prison; go ye, carry corn for the famine of your houses; ²⁰but bring your youngest brother unto me; so shall your words be verified, and ye shall not die.' And they did so.

²¹And they said one to another, 'We are verily guilty concerning our brother, in that we saw the anguish of his soul, when he besought us, and we would not hear; therefore is this distress come upon us.' ²²And Reuben answered them, saying, 'Spake I not unto you, saying, "Do not sin against the child," and ye would not hear? Therefore, behold, also his blood is required.' ²³And they knew not that Joseph understood them; for he spake unto them by an interpreter. ²⁴And he turned himself about from them, and wept; and returned to them again, and communed with them, and took from them Simeon, and bound him before their eyes.

²⁵Then Joseph commanded to fill their sacks with corn, and to restore every man's money into his sack, and to give them provision for the way: and thus did he unto them. ²⁶And they laded their asses with the corn, and departed thence. ²⁷And as one of them opened his sack to give his ass provender in the inn, he espied his money; for, behold, it was in his sack's mouth. ²⁸And he said unto his brethren, 'My money is restored; and, lo, it is even in my sack,' and their heart failed them, and they were afraid, saying one to another,

'What is this that God hath done unto us?'

²⁹And they came unto Jacob their father unto the land of Canaan, and told him all that befell unto them; saying, ³⁰'The man, who is the lord of the land, spake roughly to us, and took us for spies of the country. ³¹And we said unto him, "We are true men; we are no spies: ³²we be twelve brethren, sons of our father; one is not, and the youngest is this day with our father in the land of Canaan." ³³And the man, the lord of the country, said unto us, "Hereby shall I know that ye are true men; leave one of your brethren here with me, and take food for the famine of your households, and be gone; ³⁴and bring your youngest brother unto me: then shall I know that ye are no spies, but that ye are true men: so will I deliver you your brother, and ye shall traffick in the land."'

³⁵And it came to pass as they emptied their sacks, that, behold, every man's bundle of money was in his sack: and when both they and their father saw the bundles of money, they were afraid. ³⁶And Jacob their father said unto them, 'Me have ye bereaved of my children: Joseph is not, and Simeon is not, and ye will take Benjamin away; all these things are against me.' ³⁷And Reuben spake unto his father, saying, 'Slay my two sons, if I bring him not to thee; deliver him into my hand, and I will bring him to thee again.' ³⁸And Jacob said, 'My son shall not go down with you; for his brother is dead, and he is left alone; if mischief befall him by the way in the which ye go, then shall ye bring down my gray hairs with sorrow to the grave.'

43 And the famine was sore in the land. ²And it came to pass, when they had eaten up the corn which they had brought out of Egypt, their father said unto them, 'Go again, buy us a little food.' ³And Judah spake unto him, saying, 'The man did solemnly protest unto us, saying, "Ye shall not see my face, except your brother be with you." ⁴If thou wilt send our brother with us, we will go down and buy thee food; ⁵ but if thou wilt not send him, we will not go down; for the man said unto us, "Ye shall not see my face, except your brother be with you."' ⁶And Israel said, 'Wherefore dealt ye so ill with me, as to tell the man whether ye had yet a brother?' ⁷And they said, 'The man asked us straitly of our state, and of our kindred, saying, "Is your father yet alive? Have ye another brother?" And we told him according to the tenor of these words: could we certainly know that he would say, "Bring your brother down"?' ⁸And Judah said unto Israel his father, 'Send the lad with me, and we will arise and go; that we may live, and not die, both we, and thou, and also our little ones. ⁹ I will be surety for him; of my hand shalt thou require him; if I bring him not unto thee, and set him before thee, then let me bear the blame for ever; ¹⁰for except we had lingered, surely now we had returned this second time.' ¹¹And their father Israel said unto them, 'If it must be so now, do this; take of the best fruits in the land in your vessels, and carry down the man a present, a little balm, and a little honey, spices, and myrrh, nuts, and almonds; ¹² and take double money in your hand; and the money that was brought again in the mouth of your sacks, carry it again in your hand; peradventure it was an oversight; [13] take also your brother, and arise, go again unto the man; [14] and God Almighty give you mercy before the man, that he may send away your other brother, and Benjamin. If I be bereaved of my children, I am bereaved.'

[15] And the men took that present, and they took double money in their hand, and Benjamin; and rose up, and went down to Egypt, and stood before Joseph. [16] And when Joseph saw Benjamin with them, he said to the ruler of his house, 'Bring these men home, and slay, and make ready; for these men shall dine with me at noon.' [17] And the man did as Joseph bade; and the man brought the men into Joseph's house. [18] And the men were afraid, because they were brought into Joseph's house; and they said, 'Because of the money that was returned in our sacks at the first time are we brought in; that he may seek occasion against us, and fall upon us, and take us for bondmen, and our asses.' [19] And they came near to the steward of Joseph's house, and they communed with him at the door of the house, [20] And said, 'O sir, we came indeed down at the first time to buy food; [21] and it came to pass, when we came to the inn, that we opened our sacks, and, behold, every man's money was in the mouth of his sack, our money in full weight; and we have brought it again in our hand. [22] And other money have we brought down in our hands to buy food; we cannot tell who put our money in our sacks.' [23] And he said, 'Peace be to you, fear not: your God, and the God of your father, hath given you treasure in your sacks; I had your money.' And he brought Simeon out unto

them. ²⁴And the man brought the men into Joseph's house, and gave them water, and they washed their feet; and he gave their asses provender. ²⁵And they made ready the present against Joseph came at noon; for they heard that they should eat bread there.

²⁶And when Joseph came home, they brought him the present which was in their hand into the house, and bowed themselves to him to the earth. ²⁷And he asked them of their welfare, and said, 'Is your father well, the old man of whom ye spake? Is he yet alive?' ²⁸And they answered, 'Thy servant our father is in good health, he is yet alive.' And they bowed down their heads, and made obeisance. ²⁹And he lifted up his eyes, and saw his brother Benjamin, his mother's son, and said, 'Is this your younger brother, of whom ye spake unto me?' And he said, 'God be gracious unto thee, my son.' ³⁰And Joseph made haste; for his bowels did yearn upon his brother: and he sought where to weep; and he entered into his chamber, and wept there. ³¹And he washed his face, and went out, and refrained himself, and said, 'Set on bread.' ³²And they set on for him by himself, and for them by themselves, and for the Egyptians, which did eat with him, by themselves; because the Egyptians might not eat bread with the Hebrews; for that is an abomination unto the Egyptians. ³³And they sat before him, the firstborn according to his birthright, and the youngest according to his youth; and the men marvelled one at another. ³⁴And he took and sent messes unto them from before him; but Benjamin's mess was five times so much as any of theirs. And they drank, and were merry with him.

44 And he commanded the steward of his house, saying, 'Fill the men's sacks with food, as much as they can carry, and put every man's money in his sack's mouth. ²And put my cup, the silver cup, in the sack's mouth of the youngest, and his corn money.' And he did according to the word that Joseph had spoken. ³As soon as the morning was light, the men were sent away, they and their asses. ⁴And when they were gone out of the city, and not yet far off, Joseph said unto his steward, 'Up, follow after the men; and when thou dost overtake them, say unto them, "Wherefore have ye rewarded evil for good? ⁵Is not this it in which my lord drinketh, and whereby indeed he divineth? Ye have done evil in so doing."'

⁶And he overtook them, and he spake unto them these same words. ⁷And they said unto him, 'Wherefore saith my lord these words? God forbid that thy servants should do according to this thing; ⁸behold, the money, which we found in our sacks' mouths, we brought again unto thee out of the land of Canaan; how then should we steal out of thy lord's house silver or gold? ⁹With whomsoever of thy servants it be found, both let him die, and we also will be my lord's bondmen.' ¹⁰And he said, 'Now also let it be according unto your words: he with whom it is found shall be my servant; and ye shall be blameless.' ¹¹Then they speedily took down every man his sack to the ground, and opened every man his sack. ¹²And he searched, and began at the eldest, and left at the youngest; and the cup was found in Benjamin's sack. ¹³Then they rent their clothes, and laded every man his ass, and returned to the city.

¹⁴And Judah and his brethren came to Joseph's house; for he was yet there; and they fell before him on the ground. ¹⁵And Joseph said unto them, 'What deed is this that ye have done? Wot ye not that such a man as I can certainly divine?' ¹⁶And Judah said, 'What shall we say unto my lord? What shall we speak? Or how shall we clear ourselves? God hath found out the iniquity of thy servants: behold, we are my lord's servants, both we, and he also with whom the cup is found.' ¹⁷And Joseph said, 'God forbid that I should do so; but the man in whose hand the cup is found, he shall be my servant; and as for you, get you up in peace unto your father.'

¹⁸Then Judah came near unto him, and said, 'Oh my lord, let thy servant, I pray thee, speak a word in my lord's ears, and let not thine anger burn against thy servant; for thou art even as Pharaoh. ¹⁹My lord asked his servants, saying, "Have ye a father, or a brother?" ²⁰And we said unto my lord, "We have a father, an old man, and a child of his old age, a little one; and his brother is dead, and he alone is left of his mother, and his father loveth him." ²¹And thou saidst unto thy servants, "Bring him down unto me, that I may set mine eyes upon him." ²²And we said unto my lord, "The lad cannot leave his father; for if he should leave his father, his father would die." ²³And thou saidst unto thy servants, "Except your youngest brother come down with you, ye shall see my face no more." ²⁴And it came to pass when we came up unto thy servant my father, we told him the words of my lord. ²⁵And our father said, "Go again, and buy us a little food." ²⁶And we said, "We cannot go down: if our youngest brother be with

us, then will we go down; for we may not see the man's face, except our youngest brother be with us." ²⁷And thy servant my father said unto us, "Ye know that my wife bare me two sons; ²⁸and the one went out from me, and I said, 'Surely he is torn in pieces; and I saw him not since,' ²⁹and if ye take this also from me, and mischief befall him, ye shall bring down my gray hairs with sorrow to the grave." ³⁰Now therefore when I come to thy servant my father, and the lad be not with us; seeing that his life is bound up in the lad's life; ³¹it shall come to pass, when he seeth that the lad is not with us, that he will die; and thy servants shall bring down the gray hairs of thy servant our father with sorrow to the grave. ³²For thy servant became surety for the lad unto my father, saying, "If I bring him not unto thee, then I shall bear the blame to my father for ever." ³³Now therefore, I pray thee, let thy servant abide instead of the lad a bondman to my lord; and let the lad go up with his brethren. ³⁴For how shall I go up to my father, and the lad be not with me? Lest peradventure I see the evil that shall come on my father.'

45 Then Joseph could not refrain himself before all them that stood by him; and he cried, 'Cause every man to go out from me.' And there stood no man with him, while Joseph made himself known unto his brethren. ²And he wept aloud; and the Egyptians and the house of Pharaoh heard. ³And Joseph said unto his brethren, 'I am Joseph; doth my father yet live?' And his brethren could not answer him; for they were troubled at his presence. ⁴And Joseph said unto

his brethren, 'Come near to me, I pray you.' And they came near. And he said, 'I am Joseph your brother, whom ye sold into Egypt. ⁵Now therefore be not grieved, nor angry with yourselves, that ye sold me hither; for God did send me before you to preserve life. ⁶For these two years hath the famine been in the land; and yet there are five years, in the which there shall neither be earing nor harvest. ⁷And God sent me before you to preserve you a posterity in the earth, and to save your lives by a great deliverance. ⁸So now it was not you that sent me hither, but God; and he hath made me a father to Pharaoh, and lord of all his house, and a ruler throughout all the land of Egypt. ⁹Haste ye, and go up to my father, and say unto him, "Thus saith thy son Joseph, God hath made me lord of all Egypt: come down unto me, tarry not; ¹⁰and thou shalt dwell in the land of Goshen, and thou shalt be near unto me, thou, and thy children, and thy children's children, and thy flocks, and thy herds, and all that thou hast; ¹¹and there will I nourish thee; for yet there are five years of famine; lest thou, and thy household, and all that thou hast, come to poverty." ¹²And, behold, your eyes see, and the eyes of my brother Benjamin, that it is my mouth that speaketh unto you. ¹³And ye shall tell my father of all my glory in Egypt, and of all that ye have seen; and ye shall haste and bring down my father hither.' ¹⁴And he fell upon his brother Benjamin's neck, and wept; and Benjamin wept upon his neck. ¹⁵Moreover he kissed all his brethren, and wept upon them; and after that his brethren talked with him.

¹⁶And the fame thereof was heard in Pharaoh's house,

saying, 'Joseph's brethren are come'; and it pleased Pharaoh well, and his servants. [17]And Pharaoh said unto Joseph, 'Say unto thy brethren, "This do ye; lade your beasts, and go, get you unto the land of Canaan; [18]And take your father and your households, and come unto me; and I will give you the good of the land of Egypt, and ye shall eat the fat of the land." [19]Now thou art commanded, this do ye: "Take you wagons out of the land of Egypt for your little ones, and for your wives, and bring your father, and come. [20]Also regard not your stuff; for the good of all the land of Egypt is yours."' [21]And the children of Israel did so; and Joseph gave them wagons, according to the commandment of Pharaoh, and gave them provision for the way. [22]To all of them he gave each man changes of raiment; but to Benjamin he gave three hundred pieces of silver, and five changes of raiment. [23]And to his father he sent after this manner: ten asses laden with the good things of Egypt, and ten she asses laden with corn and bread and meat for his father by the way. [24]So he sent his brethren away, and they departed: and he said unto them, 'See that ye fall not out by the way.'

[25]And they went up out of Egypt, and came into the land of Canaan unto Jacob their father, [26]and told him, saying, 'Joseph is yet alive, and he is governor over all the land of Egypt.' And Jacob's heart fainted, for he believed them not. [27]And they told him all the words of Joseph, which he had said unto them; and when he saw the wagons which Joseph had sent to carry him, the spirit of Jacob their father revived; [28]and Israel said, 'It is enough. Joseph my son is yet alive; I will go and see him before I die.'

46 And Israel took his journey with all that he had, and came to Beer-sheba, and offered sacrifices unto the God of his father Isaac. ²And God spake unto Israel in the visions of the night, and said, 'Jacob, Jacob.' And he said, 'Here am I.' ³And God said, 'I am God, the God of thy father: fear not to go down into Egypt; for I will there make of thee a great nation; ⁴I will go down with thee into Egypt; and I will also surely bring thee up again; and Joseph shall put his hand upon thine eyes.' ⁵And Jacob rose up from Beer-sheba: and the sons of Israel carried Jacob their father, and their little ones, and their wives, in the wagons which Pharaoh had sent to carry him. ⁶And they took their cattle, and their goods, which they had gotten in the land of Canaan, and came into Egypt, Jacob, and all his seed with him: ⁷his sons, and his sons' sons with him, his daughters, and his sons' daughters, and all his seed brought he with him into Egypt.

⁸And these are the names of the children of Israel, which came into Egypt, Jacob and his sons: Reuben, Jacob's firstborn. ⁹And the sons of Reuben: Hanoch, and Phallu, and Hezron, and Carmi.

¹⁰And the sons of Simeon: Jemuel, and Jamin, and Ohad, and Jachin, and Zohar, and Shaul the son of a Canaanitish woman.

¹¹And the sons of Levi: Gershon, Kohath, and Merari.

¹²And the sons of Judah: Er, and Onan, and Shelah, and Pharez, and Zerah; but Er and Onan died in the land of Canaan. And the sons of Pharez were Hezron and Hamul.

¹³And the sons of Issachar: Tola, and Phuvah, and Job, and Shimron.

¹⁴And the sons of Zebulun: Sered, and Elon, and Jahleel. ¹⁵These be the sons of Leah, which she bare unto Jacob in Padan-aram, with his daughter Dinah: all the souls of his sons and his daughters were thirty and three.

¹⁶And the sons of Gad: Ziphion, and Haggi, Shuni, and Ezbon, Eri, and Arodi, and Areli.

¹⁷And the sons of Asher: Jimnah, and Ishuah, and Isui, and Beriah, and Serah their sister: and the sons of Beriah: Heber, and Malchiel. ¹⁸These are the sons of Zilpah, whom Laban gave to Leah his daughter, and these she bare unto Jacob, even sixteen souls. ¹⁹The sons of Rachel Jacob's wife: Joseph, and Benjamin.

²⁰And unto Joseph in the land of Egypt were born Manasseh and Ephraim, which Asenath the daughter of Potipherah priest of On bare unto him.

²¹And the sons of Benjamin were Belah, and Becher, and Ashbel, Gera, and Naaman, Ehi, and Rosh, Muppim, and Huppim, and Ard. ²²These are the sons of Rachel, which were born to Jacob: all the souls were fourteen.

²³And the sons of Dan: Hushim.

²⁴And the sons of Naphtali: Jahzeel, and Guni, and Jezer, and Shillem. ²⁵These are the sons of Bilhah, which Laban gave unto Rachel his daughter, and she bare these unto Jacob: all the souls were seven. ²⁶All the souls that came with Jacob into Egypt, which came out of his loins, besides Jacob's sons' wives, all the souls were threescore and six; ²⁷and the sons of Joseph, which were born him in Egypt, were two souls: all the souls of the house of Jacob, which came into Egypt, were threescore and ten.

²⁸And he sent Judah before him unto Joseph, to direct his face unto Goshen; and they came into the land of Goshen. ²⁹And Joseph made ready his chariot, and went up to meet Israel his father, to Goshen, and presented himself unto him; and he fell on his neck, and wept on his neck a good while. ³⁰And Israel said unto Joseph, 'Now let me die, since I have seen thy face, because thou art yet alive.' ³¹And Joseph said unto his brethren, and unto his father's house, 'I will go up, and shew Pharaoh, and say unto him, "My brethren, and my father's house, which were in the land of Canaan, are come unto me; ³²and the men are shepherds, for their trade hath been to feed cattle; and they have brought their flocks, and their herds, and all that they have." ³³And it shall come to pass, when Pharaoh shall call you, and shall say, "What is your occupation?" ³⁴That ye shall say, "Thy servants' trade hath been about cattle from our youth even until now, both we, and also our fathers," that ye may dwell in the land of Goshen; for every shepherd is an abomination unto the Egyptians.'

47 Then Joseph came and told Pharaoh, and said, 'My father and my brethren, and their flocks, and their herds, and all that they have, are come out of the land of Canaan; and, behold, they are in the land of Goshen.' ²And he took some of his brethren, even five men, and presented them unto Pharaoh. ³And Pharaoh said unto his brethren, 'What is your occupation?' And they said unto Pharaoh, 'Thy servants are shepherds, both we, and also our fathers.' ⁴They said moreover unto Pharaoh, 'For to sojourn in the

land are we come; for thy servants have no pasture for their flocks; for the famine is sore in the land of Canaan; now therefore, we pray thee, let thy servants dwell in the land of Goshen.' ⁵And Pharaoh spake unto Joseph, saying, 'Thy father and thy brethren are come unto thee; ⁶the land of Egypt is before thee; in the best of the land make thy father and brethren to dwell; in the land of Goshen let them dwell; and if thou knowest any men of activity among them, then make them rulers over my cattle.' ⁷And Joseph brought in Jacob his father, and set him before Pharaoh; and Jacob blessed Pharaoh. ⁸And Pharaoh said unto Jacob, 'How old art thou?' ⁹And Jacob said unto Pharaoh, 'The days of the years of my pilgrimage are an hundred and thirty years; few and evil have the days of the years of my life been, and have not attained unto the days of the years of the life of my fathers in the days of their pilgrimage.' ¹⁰And Jacob blessed Pharaoh, and went out from before Pharaoh.

¹¹And Joseph placed his father and his brethren, and gave them a possession in the land of Egypt, in the best of the land, in the land of Rameses, as Pharaoh had commanded. ¹²And Joseph nourished his father, and his brethren, and all his father's household, with bread, according to their families.

¹³And there was no bread in all the land; for the famine was very sore, so that the land of Egypt and all the land of Canaan fainted by reason of the famine. ¹⁴And Joseph gathered up all the money that was found in the land of Egypt, and in the land of Canaan, for the corn which they bought; and Joseph brought the money into Pharaoh's house. ¹⁵And

when money failed in the land of Egypt, and in the land of Canaan, all the Egyptians came unto Joseph, and said, 'Give us bread; for why should we die in thy presence? For the money faileth.' ¹⁶And Joseph said, 'Give your cattle; and I will give you for your cattle, if money fail.' ¹⁷And they brought their cattle unto Joseph: and Joseph gave them bread in exchange for horses, and for the flocks, and for the cattle of the herds, and for the asses; and he fed them with bread for all their cattle for that year. ¹⁸When that year was ended, they came unto him the second year, and said unto him, 'We will not hide it from my lord, how that our money is spent; my lord also hath our herds of cattle; there is not ought left in the sight of my lord, but our bodies, and our lands. ¹⁹Wherefore shall we die before thine eyes, both we and our land? Buy us and our land for bread, and we and our land will be servants unto Pharaoh; and give us seed, that we may live, and not die, that the land be not desolate.' ²⁰And Joseph bought all the land of Egypt for Pharaoh; for the Egyptians sold every man his field, because the famine prevailed over them; so the land became Pharaoh's. ²¹And as for the people, he removed them to cities from one end of the borders of Egypt even to the other end thereof. ²²Only the land of the priests bought he not; for the priests had a portion assigned them of Pharaoh, and did eat their portion which Pharaoh gave them; wherefore they sold not their lands.

²³Then Joseph said unto the people, 'Behold, I have bought you this day and your land for Pharaoh; lo, here is seed for you, and ye shall sow the land. ²⁴And it shall come to pass in

the increase, that ye shall give the fifth part unto Pharaoh, and four parts shall be your own, for seed of the field, and for your food, and for them of your households, and for food for your little ones.' ²⁵And they said, 'Thou hast saved our lives: let us find grace in the sight of my lord, and we will be Pharaoh's servants.' ²⁶And Joseph made it a law over the land of Egypt unto this day, that Pharaoh should have the fifth part; except the land of the priests only, which became not Pharaoh's.

²⁷And Israel dwelt in the land of Egypt, in the country of Goshen; and they had possessions therein, and grew, and multiplied exceedingly. ²⁸And Jacob lived in the land of Egypt seventeen years; so the whole age of Jacob was an hundred forty and seven years. ²⁹And the time drew nigh that Israel must die; and he called his son Joseph, and said unto him, 'If now I have found grace in thy sight, put, I pray thee, thy hand under my thigh, and deal kindly and truly with me; bury me not, I pray thee, in Egypt: ³⁰ but I will lie with my fathers, and thou shalt carry me out of Egypt, and bury me in their buryingplace.' And Joseph said, 'I will do as thou hast said.' ³¹And he said, 'Swear unto me.' And he sware unto him. And Israel bowed himself upon the bed's head.

48 And it came to pass after these things, that one told Joseph, 'Behold, thy father is sick,' and he took with him his two sons, Manasseh and Ephraim. ²And one told Jacob, and said, 'Behold, thy son Joseph cometh unto thee,' and Israel strengthened himself, and sat upon the bed. ³And

Jacob said unto Joseph, 'God Almighty appeared unto me at Luz in the land of Canaan, and blessed me, ⁴and said unto me, "Behold, I will make thee fruitful, and multiply thee, and I will make of thee a multitude of people; and will give this land to thy seed after thee for an everlasting possession."

⁵'And now thy two sons, Ephraim and Manasseh, which were born unto thee in the land of Egypt before I came unto thee into Egypt, are mine; as Reuben and Simeon, they shall be mine. ⁶And thy issue, which thou begettest after them, shall be thine, and shall be called after the name of their brethren in their inheritance. ⁷And as for me, when I came from Padan, Rachel died by me in the land of Canaan in the way, when yet there was but a little way to come unto Ephrath: and I buried her there in the way of Ephrath; the same is Beth-lehem.' ⁸And Israel beheld Joseph's sons, and said, 'Who are these?' ⁹And Joseph said unto his father, 'They are my sons, whom God hath given me in this place.' And he said, 'Bring them, I pray thee, unto me, and I will bless them.' ¹⁰Now the eyes of Israel were dim for age, so that he could not see. And he brought them near unto him; and he kissed them, and embraced them. ¹¹And Israel said unto Joseph, 'I had not thought to see thy face; and, lo, God hath shewed me also thy seed.' ¹²And Joseph brought them out from between his knees, and he bowed himself with his face to the earth. ¹³And Joseph took them both, Ephraim in his right hand toward Israel's left hand, and Manasseh in his left hand toward Israel's right hand, and brought them near unto him. ¹⁴And Israel stretched out his right hand, and laid

it upon Ephraim's head, who was the younger, and his left hand upon Manasseh's head, guiding his hands wittingly; for Manasseh was the first-born.

¹⁵And he blessed Joseph, and said, 'God, before whom my fathers Abraham and Isaac did walk, the God which fed me all my life long unto this day, ¹⁶the Angel which redeemed me from all evil, bless the lads; and let my name be named on them, and the name of my fathers Abraham and Isaac; and let them grow into a multitude in the midst of the earth.' ¹⁷And when Joseph saw that his father laid his right hand upon the head of Ephraim, it displeased him; and he held up his father's hand, to remove it from Ephraim's head unto Manasseh's head. ¹⁸And Joseph said unto his father, 'Not so, my father, for this is the firstborn; put thy right hand upon his head.' ¹⁹And his father refused, and said, 'I know it, my son, I know it. He also shall become a people, and he also shall be great; but truly his younger brother shall be greater than he, and his seed shall become a multitude of nations.' ²⁰And he blessed them that day, saying, 'In thee shall Israel bless, saying, "God make thee as Ephraim and as Manasseh,"' and he set Ephraim before Manasseh. ²¹And Israel said unto Joseph, 'Behold, I die; but God shall be with you, and bring you again unto the land of your fathers. ²²Moreover I have given to thee one portion above thy brethren, which I took out of the hand of the Amorite with my sword and with my bow.'

49

And Jacob called unto his sons, and said, 'Gather yourselves together, that I may tell you that which shall befall you in the last days. ² Gather yourselves together, and hear, ye sons of Jacob; and hearken unto Israel your father. ³ 'Reuben, thou art my firstborn, my might, and the beginning of my strength, the excellency of dignity, and the excellency of power: ⁴ unstable as water, thou shalt not excel; because thou wentest up to thy father's bed; then defiledst thou it: he went up to my couch.

⁵ 'Simeon and Levi are brethren; instruments of cruelty are in their habitations. ⁶ O my soul, come not thou into their secret; unto their assembly, mine honour, be not thou united; for in their anger they slew a man, and in their self-will they digged down a wall. ⁷ Cursed be their anger, for it was fierce; and their wrath, for it was cruel. I will divide them in Jacob, and scatter them in Israel.

⁸ 'Judah, thou art he whom thy brethren shall praise: thy hand shall be in the neck of thine enemies; thy father's children shall bow down before thee. ⁹ Judah is a lion's whelp: from the prey, my son, thou art gone up; he stooped down, he couched as a lion, and as an old lion; who shall rouse him up? ¹⁰ The sceptre shall not depart from Judah, nor a lawgiver from between his feet, until Shiloh come; and unto him shall the gathering of the people be. ¹¹ Binding his foal unto the vine, and his ass's colt unto the choice vine; he washed his garments in wine, and his clothes in the blood of grapes; ¹² his eyes shall be red with wine, and his teeth white with milk.

¹³ 'Zebulun shall dwell at the haven of the sea; and he shall be for an haven of ships; and his border shall be unto Zidon.

¹⁴ 'Issachar is a strong ass couching down between two

burdens; [15] and he saw that rest was good, and the land that it was pleasant; and bowed his shoulder to bear, and became a servant unto tribute.

[16] 'Dan shall judge his people, as one of the tribes of Israel. [17] Dan shall be a serpent by the way, an adder in the path, that biteth the horse heels, so that his rider shall fall backward. [18] I have waited for thy salvation, O Lord.

[19] 'Gad, a troop shall overcome him; but he shall overcome at the last.

[20] 'Out of Asher his bread shall be fat, and he shall yield royal dainties.

[21] 'Naphtali is a hind let loose: he giveth goodly words.

[22] 'Joseph is a fruitful bough, even a fruitful bough by a well; whose branches run over the wall. [23] The archers have sorely grieved him, and shot at him, and hated him; [24] but his bow abode in strength, and the arms of his hands were made strong by the hands of the mighty God of Jacob (from thence is the shepherd, the stone of Israel); [25] even by the God of thy father, who shall help thee; and by the Almighty, who shall bless thee with blessings of heaven above, blessings of the deep that lieth under, blessings of the breasts, and of the womb. [26] The blessings of thy father have prevailed above the blessings of my progenitors unto the utmost bound of the everlasting hills; they shall be on the head of Joseph, and on the crown of the head of him that was separate from his brethren.

[27] 'Benjamin shall ravin as a wolf; in the morning he shall devour the prey, and at night he shall divide the spoil.'

²⁸All these are the twelve tribes of Israel; and this is it that their father spake unto them, and blessed them; every one according to his blessing he blessed them. ²⁹And he charged them, and said unto them, 'I am to be gathered unto my people; bury me with my fathers in the cave that is in the field of Ephron the Hittite, ³⁰in the cave that is in the field of Machpelah, which is before Mamre, in the land of Canaan, which Abraham bought with the field of Ephron the Hittite for a possession of a buryingplace. ³¹There they buried Abraham and Sarah his wife; there they buried Isaac and Rebekah his wife; and there I buried Leah. ³²The purchase of the field and of the cave that is therein was from the children of Heth.' ³³And when Jacob had made an end of commanding his sons, he gathered up his feet into the bed, and yielded up the ghost, and was gathered unto his people.

50 And Joseph fell upon his father's face, and wept upon him, and kissed him. ²And Joseph commanded his servants the physicians to embalm his father; and the physicians embalmed Israel. ³And forty days were fulfilled for him; for so are fulfilled the days of those which are embalmed; and the Egyptians mourned for him threescore and ten days. ⁴And when the days of his mourning were past, Joseph spake unto the house of Pharaoh, saying, 'If now I have found grace in your eyes, speak, I pray you, in the ears of Pharaoh, saying, ⁵My father made me swear, saying, "Lo, I die; in my grave which I have digged for me in the land of Canaan, there shalt thou bury me." Now therefore let me go up, I

pray thee, and bury my father, and I will come again.' ⁶And Pharaoh said, 'Go up, and bury thy father, according as he made thee swear.'

⁷And Joseph went up to bury his father; and with him went up all the servants of Pharaoh, the elders of his house, and all the elders of the land of Egypt, ⁸and all the house of Joseph, and his brethren, and his father's house; only their little ones, and their flocks, and their herds, they left in the land of Goshen. ⁹And there went up with him both chariots and horsemen; and it was a very great company. ¹⁰And they came to the threshingfloor of Atad, which is beyond Jordan, and there they mourned with a great and very sore lamentation: and he made a mourning for his father seven days. ¹¹And when the inhabitants of the land, the Canaanites, saw the mourning in the floor of Atad, they said, 'This is a grievous mourning to the Egyptians,' wherefore the name of it was called Abel-mizraim, which is beyond Jordan. ¹²And his sons did unto him according as he commanded them; ¹³for his sons carried him into the land of Canaan, and buried him in the cave of the field of Machpelah, which Abraham bought with the field for a possession of a buryingplace of Ephron the Hittite, before Mamre.

¹⁴And Joseph returned into Egypt, he, and his brethren, and all that went up with him to bury his father, after he had buried his father.

¹⁵And when Joseph's brethren saw that their father was dead, they said, 'Joseph will peradventure hate us, and will certainly requite us all the evil which we did unto him.' ¹⁶And

they sent a messenger unto Joseph, saying, 'Thy father did command before he died, saying, [17]"So shall ye say unto Joseph: Forgive, I pray thee now, the trespass of thy brethren, and their sin; for they did unto thee evil"; and now, we pray thee, forgive the trespass of the servants of the God of thy father.' And Joseph wept when they spake unto him. [18]And his brethren also went and fell down before his face; and they said, 'Behold, we be thy servants.' [19]And Joseph said unto them, 'Fear not; for am I in the place of God? [20]But as for you, ye thought evil against me; but God meant it unto good, to bring to pass, as it is this day, to save much people alive. [21]Now therefore fear ye not: I will nourish you, and your little ones.' And he comforted them, and spake kindly unto them.

[22]And Joseph dwelt in Egypt, he, and his father's house; and Joseph lived an hundred and ten years. [23]And Joseph saw Ephraim's children of the third generation: the children also of Machir the son of Manasseh were brought up upon Joseph's knees. [24]And Joseph said unto his brethren, 'I die: and God will surely visit you, and bring you out of this land unto the land which he sware to Abraham, to Isaac, and to Jacob.' [25]And Joseph took an oath of the children of Israel, saying, 'God will surely visit you, and ye shall carry up my bones from hence.' [26]So Joseph died, being an hundred and ten years old; and they embalmed him, and he was put in a coffin in Egypt.

titles in the series